D1498059

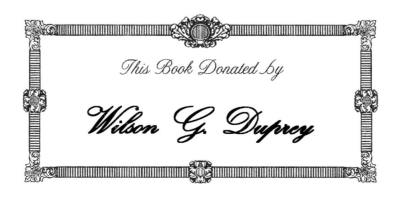

This Book Donated by

Wilson G. Duprey

CIVITATES ORBIS TERRARUM

CITIES OF THE WORLD

EUROPE and AMERICA

Introduction
by
Lelio Pagani

MAGNA BOOKS

Original title: Civitates Orbis Terrarum
Città del mondo - Europa - America
© 1990 Orsa Maggiore SpA, Torriana (FO), Italy
© English edition published by
Magna Books, Magna Road, Wigston, Leicester,
LE 8 2ZH, England.
This edition translated by Simon Knight in
association with First Edition, Cambridge.
Graphics realization by Lucchetti Editore - Bergamo,
(Italy);
Printed by GEP - Cremona, (Italy);
All rights reserved.
ISBN 1 85422 108 6

The scale and extent of urban development throughout the world is a subject of great contemporary interest. It also raises questions of how cities came into being, how they took shape and grew, what purposes they served at different stages in their growth, and what roles they have played in social, political and cultural change.

> The city is characteristic of most civilisations and is often considered their fullest expression. Its origins can be traced back beyond the 'urban revolution' which took place [...] in Mesopotamia in the third millenium BC to the archeological remains of Jericho and Catal Höyüc (Anatolia). After all these centuries, the quality of urban life is still man's central concern.[1]

When opening the pages of the work now before us — a work which appeared on the European cultural scene at the height of the Renaissance under the all-embracing title of *Civitates Orbis Terrarum* — it is almost inevitable that we should consider the significance of cities and their importance as focal points of historical and social change, or simply their great symbolic value as storehouses of a people's cultural identity and particularity.

In this introduction we will not attempt to deal with the general theme of the city and its significance but will leave the reader to exercise eye and mind in making his own way down the avenues of discovery opened to him by the individual plates and by the work as a whole. Instead, bearing in mind that the engravings are the most notable feature of the work, we will turn our attention to the way in which the city has been portrayed. And, within this broad scope — which takes in many complex disciplines[2] — we will concentrate more particularly on the image of the city 'as a realistic depiction: an objective and concrete representation of the city and its component parts'.[3]

* * *

Historically, depictions of cities over the centuries vary in significance and value, depending on the purpose which inspired the artist and his technical ability. Extant examples range from the symbolic to the realistic, and are executed in a variety of media, such as clay, stone, marble, wooden panels, walls — by means of fresco painting — and the leaves of codices.[4]

Subsequently, the dissemination of pictures of cities was greatly facilitated by the invention of printing. As a result of the new technology there are many

> books containing descriptions and illustrations, as well as [...] engravings on loose sheets produced by the proliferation of print shops which, in every town and district, strove to get down on paper a stereotyped image of their own locality, with the aim of both celebrating its virtues and documenting its unique features. Research shows that throughout Europe a growing fashion created a market for pictures of towns and cities, bringing prosperity to artisans specialised in the technique of wood engraving.[5]

Even before the invention of printing, some Renaissance codices of Ptolemy's *Geography* had included, in addition to the ancient maps of the whole world and its various regions, a series of city plans of modern inspiration. Plans of Venice, Milan, Florence, Rome, Constantinople, Damascus, Jerusalem, Cairo and Alexandria had been featured.[6] Although drawn in a kind of perspective, the cities are still represented more-or-less symbolically, not portrayed in their entirety but with the stress on their 'civic and patrician dignities'.[7]

Besides presenting images of cities, works of this kind established each city's position in a hierarchy by a selection procedure based on long historical tradition and literary associations. Even though the criteria of selection may have changed, this can help us to understand how in later works certain aspects of the city came to be featured and others played down and how some towns were given a more prominent place than others. Artistic stereotypes and literary tradition have obviously influenced the way cities are depicted and the relative importance assigned to them.[8]

The city was also a major theme in the compendia of world history which became popular towards the end of the 15th century. In these works we witness a further stage of development in the way the city was represented. Initially published with just a descriptive text, they were soon supported by a wealth of wood engravings.

It must be said, however (without going into the whole question of the relationship between truth and symbol, reality and stereotype), that the majority of these illustrations are works of pure invention and that not infrequently the same woodcuts were adapted or simply reused to make prints of different cities. On the other hand, there are also more realistic portrayals, in which the artist has been at pains to represent some of the salient features of the cities concerned. In any case, all these depictions were panoramic views rather than plans.[9]

Of special note is the *Fasciculus Temporum* by Werner Rolewinck. First published in a text-only edition at Cologne in 1474, the work was republished at Venice in 1479 featuring a number of small-scale views of cities, and later editions included a fuller series of such illustrations.[10]

Another outstanding example of a 'humanist encyclopaedia' was the *Supplementum Chronicarum* by Jacobus Philippus Foresti Bergomensis, a summary of world history 'ab initio mundi usque ad annum 1482', first published in Venice in 1482 then again in 1486 (and repeatedly throughout the 15th century), with a fine series of views of cities.[11]

A work of similar inspiration but of more impressive appearance, printed from the beginning with a wealth of illustrative material (possibly 'the first book produced mainly for its visual appeal'[12]), was the *Liber Chronicarum*, published in Latin and German by Hartmann Schedel in 1493 at Nuremberg, and consequently known as the *Nuremberg Chronicle*. It was a major undertaking 'surpassing all previous efforts in this genre in sheer size and in the number of illustrations it contained'.[13] In the *Liber*, too, the illustrations of many different cities were printed, as we have described before, from a few basic woodcuts. Such views were quite imaginary, consisting of a mixture of mainly monumental buildings, 'seen through arches and with a backdrop of strange vegetation, fanciful rivers and rugged terrain with spiky German fortifications'.[14] At least 30 of the views, though, are 'authentic', the result of close observation and reliable information. On account of the work's accurate representation of certain cities (Florence, Genoa, Venice, Rome, Jerusalem, Constantinople and, naturally, many German cities), Schedel must count as one of the pioneers of true topographical depiction of the city:

> The *Liber Chronicarum* therefore marks the beginning of a new current, a new interest in the physical aspect of the city, a change in mentality which would lead to the primacy of the graphic arts with their concern for spatial dimensions over historical narrative preoccupied with the flow of time.[15]

Works intended to collect together and popularise knowledge in this way were a response to the universalist desire to bring the whole world within the orbit of science. The process was not without conflict between old and new learning, especially in the geographical field, as man's knowledge was extended by the great voyages of discovery.

At the same time, during the 16th century, thanks partly to progress in the techniques of engraving, efforts to represent the known world systematically were becoming more refined. This tendency can be followed in detail, step by step, in the development of attempts to depict the city.[16]

An essential stage in this process, linking the 15th century tradition with later developments, was Sebastian Münster's *Cosmographia Universalis,* published in the middle years of the 16th century, a work which expressed not only its author's own interests but the universalist ambitions of a whole culture.[17]

The work is much concerned with the city and enables us to gauge changes in attitudes towards it. It has come to be seen not just as a location, a focus for learned descriptions of historical events and personalities, but as a living organism in its own right, its inner space and buildings subject to continual change.[18]

If we study early and later editions of the work and examine the relationship between its two main aspects, text and illustrations, we are also aware of a definite progression: whereas the small wood engravings of the 1544 edition are only tenuously linked to the narrative text — which in any case dwarfs the illustrations — and give a highly stylised and undifferentiated impression of the cities they are supposed to represent, the 1550 edition contains a great deal more authentic illustrative material and the individual cities — now the major theme of the work — are drawn in considerable detail:

> The city is in fact the subject of almost all the illustrations; its complexities, inner structure and component parts stand out with clarity from the page. These large-format prints break new ground in giving the city an independent identity and make us think of it in new terms.[19]

The cities in Münster's *Cosmographia* are drawn from various viewpoints, in accordance with the techniques prevailing at the time. It is interesting to note that, whereas panoramic views (realistic or imaginary) had been predominant in the 15th century 'chronicles', almost to the exclusion of other drawing techniques, in this work perspective plans are very much in evidence.[20]

It is true that woodcuts were still used for more than one city. Also, Münster had to work from originals of uneven quality and the amount of detail varies from picture to picture. Uniformity has been achieved, if at all, simply by making new woodcuts, standardising the dimensions and, if appropriate, simplifying the actual engraving.[21]

Nevertheless, the results are impressive. Quite apart from the actual content of the work, the way in which its different elements have been collected and arranged opens up promising new possibilities.

This coordination of disparate elements raises the whole question of sources. As we search for links with persons and institutions in different places, we become aware that there already existed a complex mass of interrelated material for the compiler to draw on.[22]

In considering the sources of Münster's work — and of the *Civitates* — we should remember that, in the 15th and 16th centuries, several important centres had already made considerable advances in portraying the face of the city. There were also individual artists, working in isolation, whose role was to hand or a more-or-less faithful image of one city or another, images which then became 'architypes' for later engravers to drawn on.[23]

Printing of course aided the diffusion of such works, and their dissemination was in some cases promoted by special markets such as the well-known Frankfurt book fair.[24]

There were therefore several centres of activity and a number of key meeting points (such at least was the case in Italy, Holland, Germany and France) where publishing in general and the publishing of maps and geographical material in particular had reached a certain level of sophistication.

Worthy of special mention in this context is the Roman publishing enterprise of Antonio Lafréry, who specialised in engraving plans of cities and played an important role in circulating and distributing high-quality products, both individual engravings and his famous 'collections'.[25]

Lafréry's work, like Münster's *Cosmographia*, is vital to our understanding of that stage of 'cultural growth during which the image of the city [...] was established as a separate genre and came to have its own effective means of expression'.[26]

In this cursory examination of some of the main developments in publishing, we should not overlook works concerned with the geography of particular countries. Some of these also describe, through the medium of text and illustration, the principal cities to be found in those regions, and make their own special contribution to the art of depicting the city.[27]

Thus, certain works devoted wholly or partly to describing newly discovered parts of the world were instrumental in making available depictions of cities not previously known. For instance, Temistitan (Mexico City) is illustrated in Benedetto Bordone's *Isolario,* published in Venice in 1528, and 'Cuscho, chief city of the Province of Peru' is shown in the third volume of G.B. Ramu-

sio's extraordinary work *Navigationi et Viaggi,* printed in 1556, also in Venice.[28]

To this incomplete list we could also add works on cities and fortresses in different countries, of the kind produced by A. du Pinet or G. Ballino.[29]

But by far and away the greatest 16th century work concerned exclusively with the city is that known as the *Civitates Orbis Terrarum.* It is a worthy monument to the publisher's art, of enormous value in its own right and as a milestone in the history of how the city has been depicted. Its quality and sheer scope place it among those works which transcend the times and places which gave them birth.

R.V. Tooley quite rightly asserts that 'the *Civitates* is one of the great books of the world' and that, though foreshadowed in some respects by works such as the *Nuremberg Chronicle,* Münster's *Cosmographia,* or Brydenbach's *Journeys,* it is the first serious attempt to give graphic representations of the main cities of the world, with a wealth of factual detail.[30]

The *Cosmographia* had been a first attempt at systemisation. Only twenty-two years later, in a maturer cultural context, those ambitions found a more complete expression in a fully-integrated programme of the widest scope.

If we examine the thematic basis of the work and consequently the illustrative material, we are also aware of a change. Whereas the cities in the earlier works mentioned were treated in more or less depth, but always in the context of a diversity of subject matter (the works were, after all, compendia or chronicles), in the *Civitates* the dominant, indeed the only, theme is the city itself.

*   *   *

Ambitious in conception, the *Civitates* is one of the most notable publications of the 16th century and a milestone in the history of cartography.

R.V. Tooley picks out three works in this field as outstanding for their broad scope and high quality: the first modern world atlas, the *Theatrum Orbis Terrarum* published at Antwerp by Abraham Ortelius; the first marine atlas, the *Spieghel der Zeevaert,* published at Leiden by Lucas Jansz Waghenaer; and the *Civitates Orbis Terrarum,* the first standardised collection of printed plans of the world's cities. It is also his stated opinion that the last of these was the most demanding and complex undertaking of the three.[31]

There are striking affinities between two of these works, the *Theatrum* and the *Civitates*: not only in the mutual borrowings and obvious cross-fertilisation, but also in the motives underlying the two works, their conception and growth, and the relationship between the authors, as well as a number of obvious features in their presentation.

With his *Theatrum,* published in 1570, Ortelius, indisputably one of the most authoritative geographers and cosmographers of the Renaissance,[32] had drawn the century's geographical knowledge together into a single, comprehensive volume. This was the culmination of a period during which he and his contemporaries had pursued their researches back over the centuries to reassess with an open mind the works of the ancient geographers and had also given their attention to the knowledge becoming available of the extent of the earth and its land and ocean masses. New discoveries had radically altered contemporary notions of the earth's dimensions and outline. The *Theatrum* also concluded a long process whereby the work of Ptolemy was gradually displaced from its pre-eminent position.[33] The Alexandrian geographer had been restored to a place of great authority in Western culture at the beginning of the 15th century and had continued to exercise a strong influence during the 16th century, even though his work no longer fitted the newly emerging understanding of the world.[34]

The *Theatrum* nonetheless preserved some features of Ptolemy's *Geography,* retaining, as well as its universal purpose, a similar relationship between text and maps and the same arrangement of the material. It therefore formed a bridge between the ancient model and the tradition of atlas-making of which the *Theatrum* was the first exemplar.

In Ortelius' work, as in Ptolemy's, the general maps are presented first, followed by the regional ones:

> His subiecimus harum partium singulas regiones ab occiden-taliore Europae parte exorsi, Ptolemaeum Geographorum Prin-cipem et coeteros poenes omnes imitati.[35]

It would not be inappropriate to say that Ortelius' atlas was the inspiration for the complementary work on cities before us here: from drawings of the world itself to the world's cities.

In the 16th century there was a great upsurge of interest in the city, not only in its political, economic and social aspects, but also from the point of view of culture and travel. Along the roads between one European city and another journeyed merchants, scholars and travellers, moving with a new curiosity and greater freedom to a wider range of destinations.[36] In parallel there developed a new literature of travel books and historical and geographical guides, of various shapes and sizes, which proliferated particularly in Italy, Germany, France and Holland.

Some of these books were written for the benefit of the arm-chair traveller, who could visit far-away places in imagination, comfortably installed at home without needing to face the hard-ships of life on the road.

And it was the city, 'the seat and symbol of organised social life and the focal point of trade',[37] which had first claim on the attention of traveller and reader.

We must bear in mind advances in map-making techniques, which were bound to influence the way cities were depicted,[38] and also progress in the art of engraving, particularly the engrav-ing of copper plates.[39]

> All these strands — social and political, technological, artistic — are woven into the fabric of the *Civitates Orbis Terrarum,* which [...] remains [the] most original and magnificent of all city atlases. Its compilers were the first to apply the systematic atlas-form, devised by Ortelius, to a collection of plans and views, that is, in the field of chorography; they were able to draw on the work of accomplished topographical artists; and they reproduced it in pictorial compositions of great charm and individuality.[40]

The title *Civitates Orbis Terrarum,* specifically applied to the work published in 1572, was commonly used to denote the whole collection of six volumes published over a timespan of almost 50 years between 1572 and 1618.[41]

Whereas the *Theatrum* is an almost solo effort on the part of Ortelius, the volumes of the *Civitates* are very definitely 'the result of teamwork'.[42] The two personalities who immediately spring to mind are Georg Braun and Franz Hogenberg.

The name of Hogenberg (a native of Malines, 1540-90) is also to be found in the *Theatrum.* In concluding the preface to his work, Abraham Ortelius commends to his readers the work of the engraver: 'Francisci Hogenbergii artificiosae manui, cuius unius indefatigabili diligentia fere omnes hae tabulae coelatae sunt, bene faveto'.[43] This mention is ample proof that Hogenberg worked alongside Ortelius and is testimony to his ability in the art of engraving plates for maps.[44]

Some scholars assume that it was Hogenberg who first had the idea of compiling a volume dedicated entirely to cities. In a letter from G. Braun in Cologne to Abraham Ortelius in Antwerp, dated 31 October 1571, there is in fact an early reference to the work, described as 'M. Francisci de Civitatibus librum' (Mr Fran-cis' book about cities).[45] Without going into the question of who contributed what in planning and structuring the *Civitates* — a subject on which there are many gaps in our knowledge — we are bound to recognise that Franz Hogenberg shares a place with Georg Braun as co-editor of the immortal work.

Georg Braun (or Bruin) (1541-1622) was a native of Cologne, where as a canon he enjoyed a position of authority and a living from the church.[46] His part in the creation of the *Civitates* is

different from Hogenberg's, but complementary. Whereas Hogenberg was the technician, Braun was the man of learning, with cultural and political contacts at home and abroad. His specific task was to coordinate the material and edit the historical and descriptive text, a role of increasing importance as later volumes came to be published.

In the imperial privilege for the publication of the work, granted at Vienna on 28 August 1572, a third name figures along-side those of Hogenberg and Braun: Simon vandem Noeuel (Simon Novellanus or Neuvelt), another engraver, also from Malines, who shared the work with his better-known colleague Hogenberg.[47]

The poem by A. Grapheus printed in the introductory pages of the *Civitates* gives confirmation of the different roles played by the members of this team: Braun is introduced as the author of the commentaries accompanying the plates, while the others are named as having executed the engravings ('praeclarus uterque arte Novellanus, bonus Hogenbergus').[48]

There is also a clear reference to the part each played in Braun's preface, where he praises the 'artificiosae Simonis Novel-lani et Francisci Hogenbergij manus' and then speaks of his own 'enarrationes', stating that he has drawn on various authoritative correspondents and ancient and modern writers.[49]

At the end of the preface, Braun also acknowledges the con-tribution of others, warmly thanking them for their help in vari-ous areas. One contributor he names is 'Georgius Hoefnagel An-verpianus', who had made available plates of the Iberian Region ('et accuratos Hispanicarum urbium typos') and was to play an im-portant part in supplying illustrative material for later volumes in the series.[50]

In requesting the collaboration of artists and scholars who might wish to enter into correspondence and add to the number of plans and the information relating to the various cities, Braun takes the opportunity to express his debt of gratitude to Abraham Ortelius:

> Ita opus nostrum mirifice, multarum urbium genuina descrip-tione ornavit, Praestantissimus, Doctissimusque vir, D. Abra-hamus Ortelius Anverpianus, hoc nostro tempore insignis Cos-mographus, quo optimos quosque honestis litterarum studijs faventes, maximo beneficio affecit.[51]

Ortelius' presence behind the scenes is further confirmed by a number of letters which reveal the extent and nature of his col-laboration in the creation of the *Civitates.*[52]

* * *

The names of Braun, Hogenberg and Novellanus appear in volumes I (1572), II (1575) and IV (1588). Novellanus is inex-plicably absent from volume III (1581). After the deaths of both Hogenberg and Novellanus around 1590, Braun alone put his sig-nature to the fifth volume (c. 1598). By the time the sixth volume appeared, Braun too was dead. Instead, the final volume bears the name of Abraham Hogenberg, thought to be the son of Franz.[53]

Though produced over such a long span of time, the six volumes clearly make up a single entity, one in their overall struc-ture, content and forms, and in the quality of the illustrations.[54]

In essence, each volume is still in fact a 'collection' of exist-ing material, even though the material has been subjected to care-ful analysis and a rigorous selection process. The various plans and views have been standardised in their presentation and arranged in order, but the actual drawing has not been altered in any way. This means that the work can be enjoyed simply as a review of different cities or studied as a compendium of different tech-niques of draughtsmanship.[55]

The volumes are in folio format and are all laid out in similar style: introductory texts and commendations at the beginning (with the exception of volumes V and VI), followed by a splendid sequence of plates and the accompanying 'enarrationes'.

The frontispiece to each volume is a prominent feature, a work of art in itself, which also conveys a specific message, in keeping with the volume's content and usually related to the theme of the introductory texts.[56]

The second, fourth and fifth volumes also features ample indices, generally augmented by full-scale descriptive passages; the sixth has two general indices encompassing the content of the work as a whole.

The frame of reference of each volume is the whole world (even though the bulk of the cities depicted are European). The individual volumes are not devoted to certain parts of the world so that, taken together, they give a complete picture of the whole. Rather, the volumes, though linked, are in some ways indepedent of one another, each introducing a miscellany of cities from all parts of the Earth.

There is a total of over 360 plates, distributed fairly evenly among the six volumes.

Altogether, 546 cities are represented. Some plans and views occupy a whole plate and take up a double page, others a subdivision of the whole.[57]

The volume which concerns us here consists of 58 plates including depictions of no fewer than 139 cities.

The mention of these numbers gives an idea of the immensity of the task of comparing, selecting and putting together the material which went into the work. As it is, the *Civitates* is a vast compendium of graphic images of the city, and has played a unique role in handing down pictures of the world's major cities and of many lesser ones.

The undertaking was crowned with success and the work immediately found favour with a wide readership. Reprints and translations of the early volumes were already appearing before the final volumes was published.[58]

Given the wide circulation of the work and its comprehensive body of illustrations, the *Civitates* was instrumental in forming

a basis of a common urban culture founded on the visual image: from that time on it was possible, in fact inevitable, that cities would be thought of as belonging to a universal category and as individual examples of it. For the first time, even very small cities or cities situated on the furthest fringes of the known world could take their places on this skilfully devised stage.[59]

Lelio Pagani

NOTE

1) M. Roncayolo, *La città, Storia e problemi della dimensione urbana,* Turin, 1988, 2nd edition, p. 3.

2) G.P. Caprettini, writing under the heading 'Immagine', in *Enciclopedia* Einaudi, Turin, 1979, VII, pp. 93-115; S. Alpers, *Arte del descrivere. Scienza e pittura nel Seicento olandese,* Italian translation, Turin, 1984; L. Gambi, 'L'immagine della città', *Cenobio,* XXXIV, 4, Oct-Dec 1985, pp. 284-314. For different methods of representation, it is also worth consulting J. Schulz, 'The Printed Plans and Panoramic Views of Venice, 1486-1797', in *Saggi e memorie di Storia dell'Arte, VII,* Florence, 1970: the author draws a distinction between perspective plans, topographical plans and panoramic views. See also the introduction to G. Cassini's volume *Piante e vedute prospettiche di Venezia, 1479-1855,* Venice, 1982, pp. 1-31.

3) L. Gambi, *op. cit.,* pp. 297-98.

4) See L. Gambi's introduction to 'La città da immagine simbolica a proiezione urbanistica', in *Storia d'Italia, VI,* Atlas, Turin, 1976, pp. 217-28; E. Zinner, 'Cosmologia e Cartografia', in *Enciclopedia universale dell'arte,* vol. III, Venice/Rome, 1971, pp. 864-72.

5) C. De Seta, 'Significati e simboli della rappresentazione topografica negli Atlanti dal XVI al XVII secolo', in *Città Capitali,* edited by the author, Rome/Bari, 1985, p. 20.

6) A good example is Codex Vat. Lat. 5699, kept in the Biblioteca Apostolica Vaticana. The work includes an illustration of Florence dated 1469 and the names of Ugo de Cominellis and Pietro del Massaio. For comment, see R. Almagià, *Monumenta Cartografica Vaticana, I; Planisferi, carte nautiche e affini dal secolo XIV al XVII esistenti nella Biblioteca Apostolica Vaticana,* Vatican City, 1944, p. 99. For details of other codices, see pp. 99-100.

7) L. Gambi, 'L'immagine...', p. 299. The depictions in fact include 'public buildings, churches and convents, patrician houses [...] set in empty space, abruptly surrounded by the city wall and its gates. Urban dwellings unrelated to the civil or ecclesiastical power effectively do not exist'. *(Ibid).* Noteworthy depictions of cities in manuscript works can be found in codices by Fra Paolino Minorita and Goro Dati, and also in the *Liber Insularum Archipelagi* (from the 1420s) by Cristoforo Buondelmonti. On this subject, see R. Almagià, *op. cit.,* pp. 105-17. His comments on Codex Chig. F.V. 110 *(Ibid.,* p. 110) are especially pertinent.

8) G. Ricci, 'Cataloghi di città, stereotipi etnici e gerarchie urbane nell'Italia di antico regime', *Storia Urbana,* 18, 1982, pp. 3-33; G. Fasoli, 'La coscienza civica nelle *laudes civitatum,* in *La coscienza cittadina nei comuni italiani del Duecento,* Todi, 1972, pp. 10-44; L. Gambi, 'Per una rilettura di Biondo e Alberti, geografi', in *Il Rinascimento nelle corti padane; Società e cultura,* Bari, 1977, pp. 259-75.

9) On the relationship between reality and stereotype an authoritative writer is E. Gombrich, *Art and Illusion,* Italian translation, Turin, 1965, pp. 81-111.

10) Essling (Prince d'), *Les livres à figures vénetiens de la fin du XVe siècle et du commencement du XVIe,* I, Florence, 1907, n. 276; G. Cassini, *op. cit.,* p. 33; T. Campbell, *The Earliest Printed Maps, 1472-1500,* London, 1987, pp. 142-3.

11) For information on J. Ph. Foresti, see E. Pianetti, 'Fra Jacopo Filippo Foresti e la sua opera nel quadro della cultura bergamasca, *Bergomum,* 1939, pp. 100-9 and 147-74. His *Supplementum* was reprinted several times, with additions to the illustrative material, between 1483 and 1581. See also Essling, *op. cit.,* I, n. 343; G. Cassini, *op. cit.* p. 38; T. Campbell, *op. cit.,* p. 220.

12) C. De Seta, *op. cit.,* p. 23.

13) D. Ferrari, *Mantova nelle stampe,* Brescia, 1985, p. 5. The *Chronicle* was the fruit of collaboration between the accomplished typographer Anton Koberger and the engravers Michael Wolgemut (teacher of Dürer) and Wilhelm Pleidenwurff. Such was its success that it was reprinted in 1496 and again in 1497. See also V. von Loga, 'Die Städtansichten in Hartmann Schedels Welt-chronik' *Jahrbuch der Preuss. Kunstsammlungen,* IX, 1988, pp. 93ff and 184ff; E Rüscher, *Die Schedelsche Weltchronik: Das grösste Buchunternehmen der Dürer-Zeit,* Munich, 1973; F. Bachmann, *Die Alten Stadtbilder: ein Verzeichnis der geographischen Ortansichten von Schedel bis Merian,* Leipzig, 1939, pp. 3-4; C. De Seta, *op. cit.,* pp. 23-26.

14) L. Gambi, M.C. Gozzoli, *Milano* in the series 'Le città nella storia d'Italia', Bari/Rome, 1982 p. 43.

15) C. De Seta, *op. cit.,* p. 25.

16) L. Nuti, 'Alle origini del «Grand Tour»: immagini e cultura della città italiana negli atlanti e nelle cosmografie del secolo XVI', *Storia Urbana,* 27, 1984, pp. 4-5.

17) *Ibid.* First published in German at Basel in 1541, the *Cosmographia* was soon being read by a vast public. It was translated into Latin (1550), French (1552) and Italian (1558), and updated editions continued to appear until 1628. For information about Münster himself, see: K.H. Burmeister, *Sebastian Münster: Versuch eines biographischen Gesamtbildes,* Basel/Stuttgart, 1963; R. Almagià, writing under the heading 'Münster, Sebastian' in *Enciclopedia Cattolica,* VIII, Vatican City, 1952, col. 1519. For comments on the *Cosmographia* and in particular its depictions of cities, see L. Nuti, *op. cit.,* pp. 5-12; A. De Seta, *op. cit.,* pp. 26-37.

18) L. Nuti, *op. cit.,* p. 6.

19) *Ibid.,* p. 7.

20) In analysing the various ways in which the cities are depicted, C. De Seta distinguishes the following basic models; 1) drawings which start from a ground plan and on it build an infrastructure of elementary symbols — a simplified perspective elevation, unconcerned with the architectural features of individual buildings, except for the major churches and palaces (in the 1550 edition, the illustrations of Naples, Paris, Amsterdam, Zurich and Cagliari come into this category); 2) perspective drawings in the Renaissance tradition (those of Florence, Rome, Venice, Constantinople, Geneva, Marburg, Frankfurt, etc.); 3) drawings made from ground level giving a flat silhouette of the city with all the architectural and landscape features compressed into the horizontal plane (Worms, Lübeck, Cologne, etc.). The illustration of Augsburg does not fit into any of these categories: various parts of the town are drawn in plan format showing the main civic and ecclesiastical structures but omitting the lesser buildings (C. De Seta, *op. cit.*, pp. 38-46). Also of interest is F. Danville, *La géographie des Humanistes*, Paris, 1940, and by the same author, *Le langage des géographes*, Paris, 1964; N. Broc, *La Géographie de la Renaissance (1429-1620)*, Paris, 1979.

21) Unlike the anonymous illustrations of the first edition, the new engravings bore the initials of specific draughtsmen and engravers.

22) L. Nuti, *op. cit.*, pp. 9-11, gives details of the plans of Italian cities represented in the *Cosmographia* and their probable source materials.

23) Without considering other countries, Italian cities such as Florence, Venice, Rome and others, already had traditions of this kind. While it is worth turning to specific studies for the history of how individual cities have been depicted, R.V. Tooley gives an overall view in 'Maps in Italian Atlases of the Sixteenth Century (being a Comparative List of the Italian Maps Issued by Lafreri, Forlani, Duchetti, Bertelli and Others, found in Atlases)', *Imago Mundi*, III, 1939, pp. 12-47.

24) It is interesting to study the official catalogue of the Frankfurt book fair published in 1573 by Georg Willer (L. Bagrow, 'A Page in the History of the Distribution of Maps', *Imago Mundi*, v, 1948, pp. 53-62). For information on map production, see R.A. Skelton, *Decorative Printed Maps of the 15th to 18th Century: A Revised Edition of 'Old Decorative Maps and Charts', by A.L. Humphreys*, London/New York, 1952; R.V. Tooley, *op. cit.*; R. Almagià, *Monumenta Cartografica Vaticana, II, Carte geografiche a stampa di particolare pregio o rarità dei secoli XVI e XVII esistenti nella Biblioteca Apostolica Vaticana*, Vatican City, 1948.

25) For information on Antonio Lafréry, the map-seller whose Rome workshop was for many years (1544-77) the centre of a flourishing trade, see F. Ehrle, *Roma prima di Sisto V; La pianta di Roma du Perac-Lafréry del 1577*, Rome, 1908. For an evaluation of his 'collections', arranged in the Ptolemaic sequence, with the addition of plans of cities and fortresses, see O. Baldacci, 'Introduzione ad una mostra di atlanti antichi', and M. La Corte, 'Catalogo di raccolte fattizie e di atlanti dei secoli XVI-XVII', both in *XX Congr. Geogr. Roma 1967, Mostra di tolomei e atlanti antichi*, Rome, Italian Geographical Society, 1967; also of interest is L. Pagani, 'Una raccolta di carte geografiche del secolo XVI', *Bergomum*, LXXIII (1-2), Jan.-July 1979, pp. 3-67. For further information on Lafréry and other engraver/printers of the period, see R.V. Tooley, *Maps and Map-makers*, London, 1978, 6th edition, pp. 20-21.

26) L. Nuti, *op. cit.*, p. 11.

27) It is well worth referring to works such as the *Schwzer Chronik* by Johann Stumpf (1548) or the *Descrittione di tutti i Paesi Bassi* by Lodovico Giucciardini (1567) 'containing several geographical maps of the country and realistic drawings of a number of the principal cities'.

28) B. Bordon, *Libro nel qual si ragiona di tutte l'isole del mondo*, Venice, 1528 (for a critical appreciation, see M. Billanovich's article 'Benedetto Bordon' in *Dizionario Biografico degli Italiani, VII*, Rome, 1970, pp. 511-13); G.B. Ramusio, *Navigationi et Viaggi*, Venice, 3 volumes, 1550-59 [?]: the reference to 'Cuscho' is in the third volume, 1556, pp. 411-12 (For comment see M. Milanesi, *Tolomeo sostituito; Studi di storia delle conoscenze geografiche nel XVII secolo*, Milan, 1984, or the same writer's essays commenting on the edition of Ramusio's work, Einaudi, Turin, 1978-85).

29) A. Du Pinet, *Plantz, pourtraitz et descriptions de plusieurs villes et forteresses tant de l'Europe, Asie, Afrique, que des Indes et terres neuves; leurs fondations, antiquitez et manieres de vivre, avec plusieurs cartes...*, Lyon, 1564; G. Ballino, *Dei disegni delle più illustri città e fortezze del mondo*, Venice, 1569.

30) From R.V. Tooley's Preface to G. Braun and F. Hogenberg, *Civitates Orbis Terrarum, The Towns of the World, 1572-1618*, with an Introduction by R.A. Skelton, Cleveland, New York, 1966, vol. I, p. V.

31) *Ibid.*.

32) J. Denuce, *Oud Nederlandse Kaartmakers in betrekking met Plantijn*, 1912 reprinted Amsterdam, 1964; C. Koeman, 'The History of Abraham Ortelius and his *Theatrum Orbis Terrarum*', Introduction to the 1570 facsimile edition, Lausanne, 1964; R.A. Skelton, 'Abraham Ortelius, The Theatre of the Whole World', Facsimile of the 1606 English Edition, Amsterdam, 1968; R.V. Tooley, *Maps and Map-makers*, pp. 29-30; R. Almagià, writing under the heading 'A. Ortelio', in the *Enciclopedia Italiana;* U. Thieme and F. Becker, *Allgemeines Lexikon der bildenden Künstler von der Antike bis zur Gegenwart*, XIX, Leipzig; M. van den Broecke, 'Facts and Speculations on the Production and Survival of Ortelius' *Theatrum Orbis Terrarum* and its Maps, *The Map Collector*, 26, Sept. 1986, pp. 2-12.

33) M. Milanesi, *Tolomeo sostituito...*, pp. 9-24.

34) For a list of the various editions of Ptolemy's *Geographia*, consult R.V. Tooley, 'Maps and Map-makers', pp. 6-8. For information on the manuscript tradition, see J. Fischer, *Claudii Ptolemaei Geographiae Codex Urbinas Graecus 82*, especially the preliminary volume, and *De Claudii Ptolemaei vita operibus Geographia praesertim eiusque fatis*, Leiden/Leipzig, 1932.

35) A. Ortelius, *Theatrum Orbis Terrarum*, Antwerp, 1570, preface. The 1570 edition has a sumptuous frontispiece with allegorical figures representing the continents (Europe at the top, Asia and Africa at the sides, America at the bottom). This is followed by an 'Explicatio' in verse by 'A. Moekerchii brugensis', the author's preface and a most valuable 'Catalogus Auctorum tabularum geographicarum' (for comment, see L. Bagrow, *A. Ortelii Catalogus Cartographorum*, Gotha, 1928-30). The individual plates are accompanied by descriptive texts, each of which is followed by details which ancient and modern authors had written about the region in question. Also of great value are the notes provided by Arnoldus Mylius, at the foot of the page, setting out the ancient place names and their modern equivalents and the same information in reverse.

36) R.A. Skelton, Introduction to G. Braun and F. Hogenberg, *Civitates...*, p.. VII; C. De Seta, 'L'Italia nello specchio del «Grand Tour», in *Storia d'Italia, Annali, V, Il Paesaggio'*, Turin, 1982, pp. 125-263.

37) R.A. Skelton, Introduction, p. VII.

38) L. Bagrow, *History of Cartography*, enlarged by R.A. Skelton, London, 1964; N. Broc and E. Guidoni, 'La rivoluzione delle immagini', in E. Guidoni and A. Marino *Storia dell'urbanistica, Il Cinquecento*, Rome/Bari, 1982, pp. 110-81; L. Gambi, 'La città...'.

39) P. Colin, *La gravure et les graveurs*, Brussels, 1916-18; A. Petrucci, *Panorama dell'incisione italiana. Il Cinquecento*, 1964; L. Firpo, 'Immagine e potere', in AA.VV. *I rami incisi dell'Archivio di Corte: sovrani, battaglie, architetture, topografie*, Turin, 1981.

40) R.A. Skelton, Introduction, p. VII.

41) *Ibid.*, p. X and Appendix A: 'Printing-History of the *Civitates*, 1572-1618, pp. XXIV-XXVII; F. Bachmann, *op. cit.*, pp. 7-10; J. Denuce, *op. cit.*.

42) R.V. Tooley, Preface, p. V.

43) A. Ortelius, *op. cit.*, preface.

44) For further information on Hogenberg, see F. Bachmann, *op. cit.*, pp. 6-9; C. Koeman, 'The History...'; R.A. Skelton, Introduction, p. IX; U. Thieme and F. Becker, *op. cit.* XVII, 1924, pp. 306-7.

45) The letter (now in the British Museum, Harley 7011, fol. 167) is reproduced in A. Popham's 'Georg Hoefnagel and the *Civitates Orbis Terrarum, Maso Finiguerra*, I (2-3), 1936, pp. 185-7.

46) For further information about Braun, the following works are of interest: H. Lempertz, 'Städtebuch von Georg Braun und Franz Hogenberg und die darin enthaltene Anbildung und Beschreibung Werdens', *Annalen des Historischen Vereins für den Niederrhein*, XXXVI, 1881, pp. 179-86; E. Wiepen, 'Bartholomäus Bruyn der Ältere und Georg Braun', *Jahrbuch des Kölnischen Geschichtsvereins*, III, 1916, pp. 95-153; F. Bachmann, *op. cit.*, p. 7; R.A. Skelton, Introduction, p. VIII.

47) For information on Novellanus, see F. Bachmann, *op. cit.*, p. 7; R.A. Skelton, Introduction, pp. VIII-IX; U. Thieme and F. Becker *op. cit.*, XXV, 1931, p. 529.

48) *Civitates Orbis Terrarum*, Cologne, 1572, 'Explicatio', by A. Grapheus.

49) *Ibid.*, Braun's preface. In referring to his 'historicae enarrationes', Braun (in the preface to the third volume) says that they have been woven together 'optima fide ex veterum et recentiorum scriptis, ex communicatis doctissimorum virorum sermonibus et literis, ex observatione demum propria'.

50) The following works contain further information on Hoefnagel: A. Popham, *op. cit.;* E. Fétis, 'Les artistes belges à l'étranger: Georges Hoefnagel', *Bulletin de l'Académie Royale des Sciences, des Lettres et des Beaux-Arts de Belgique*, XXI, 1854, pp. 978-1012; R.A. Skelton, Introduction, pp. XI-XIV; E. Chmelarz, 'Georg und Jakob Hoefnagel' *Jahrbuch der Kunsthistorischen Sammlungen des Alerh. Kaiserhauses*, XVII, 1896, pp. 275-90; U. Thieme and F. Becker, XVII, pp. 193-95; F. Bachmann, *op. cit.*, p. 7. The other artists thanked for their contributions are: Cornelius Chaymox, who supplied plates of some German cities; Constantinius Liskirchius for depictions of 'earum urbium oppidorumque [...] quae ex Africa, Asia, et India pauci ante depictas viderunt'; and finally Gerardus à Grosbek and Gregorius Sylvius for the plan of the city of Liège (Preface to the *Civitates*).

51) Also from the preface to the *Civitates*.

52) Ortelius facilitated the task of collecting together the illustrations through his contacts with collaborators and scholars all over Europe. The *Theatrum* and the *Civitates* were associated in people's minds and sometimes confused. See A. Popham, *op. cit.*, pp. 189 ff. The words *Orbis Terrarum* in the titles of both works, referring to their scope, also formed an obvious link. As regards the correspondence between Braun and Ortelius, in addition to the 1571 letter quoted earlier (reproduced by Popham), a second letter in 1572 and others written in 1580 and 1595 are of interest (reproduced in a work edited by J.H. Hessels, *Ecclesiae Londino-Batavae Archivum, I, Abrahami Ortelii geographi antverpiensis et virorum eruditorum... epistulae*, Cambridge, 1887, under numbers 37, 96, 178, 217, 239, 240, 258, 263, 272). See also the descriptive text on Antwerp in the *Civitates* itself.

53) R.A. Skelton, Introduction, p. VIII; U. Thieme and F. Becker, *op. cit.*, XVII, 1924, p. 308.

54) The title *Civitates Orbis Terrarum*, which came to be used to describe the work as a whole, was in fact given only to the first volume. The later volumes were entitled: 'De praecipuis totius universi urbibus liber secundus'; 'Urbium praecipuarum totius mundi liber tertius'; 'Liber quartus urbium praecipuarum totius mundi'; 'Urbium praecipuarum mundi theatrum quintum'; 'Theatri praecipuarum totius mundi liber sextus'.

55) L. Nuti, *op. cit.*, p. 15.

56) For example, the frontispiece to the first volume features allegorical figures celebrating architecture, thereby alluding to the theme of Braun's preface; the frontispiece to the second, which shows Cybele, Great Mother of the Gods, and figures of 'Religio' and 'Politia', Lares and Penates, also heralds the volume's preface, again by Braun, who takes as his theme the foundation and history of cities. Similar connections are evident in the subsequent volumes.

57) R.A. Skelton, Introduction, Appendix B, 'Classified List of Plans and Views', pp. XXVIII - XLIII.

58) For information on the complex history of the *Civitates* and its various editions, refer to the works mentioned in note 41. The French edition was entitled *Théâtre des cités du monde* or *Théâtre des principales villes de tout l'Univers*, or variants of these; the German edition was named *Beschreibung und Contrafactur der vornehmster Städte der Welt.*

59) L. Nuti, *op. cit.*

LIST OF PLATES

* This volume contains 29 of the 58 plates from G. Braun and F. Hogenberg's *Civitates Orbis Terrarum,* published by Th. Gramineus of Cologne in 1572. For the sake of completeness, a list of the remaining plates, reproduced in the same way in a separate volume entitled *Civitates Orbis Terrarum, Cities of the World; Europe - Africa - Asia,* is given below.

The plates are reproduced from an original preserved in the Biblioteca Civica A. Mai at Bergamo, accession number Cinq. 7. 761. The hand colouring of this copy is particularly fine and clear.

A full facsimile edition of this magnificent work, with an introduction by Luigi Chiodi, was made in 1977.

We would like to express our sincere thanks to the Director of the Biblioteca Civica, Bergamo, for allowing us to reproduce the plates and so make them more widely known.

TABVLAE

POS TERI TAT

CON SVL TV

ORNAMENT. ORB. TERR.

CIVITA TES OR BIS TER RARVM

ARCIVM INVENTRIX.

OPIDOR. AVCTOR.

CONSOCIAT. HVMANI GEN. ORIGO.

ARCHITECT. RVDIM.

DOMICIL. TYROCIN.

LONDINVM FER
GLIAE REGN

Clarkenwell

Smythe
Fyeld.

S. Gyles in
the ffelde.

Hew Borne

Chart
hiure

Suffolke P.   Durisme P.
Somer set Place.   Arundell P.
Beere house   Savoy
The Corte   The Temple   Whyt freres
                                                                              Bridwell   Blak freres   Bena
Paris bredge

Lamberth Mar
hei

West
Mester

Sterre Chamber

Y Quenes
Bredge

Paris Gard̄en

The Slaugh
ter howse

Lamberth

Hæc est Regia illa totius Angliæ ciuitas LONDINVM, ad fluuium Thamesin sita. Cæsari, vt plures exis timat, Trinobantum
nuncupata, multarum gentium cōmercio nobilitata, exculta domib. ornata tē-
plis, excelsa arcibus, claris ingenijs, viris omnium artium doctrinarumq, gene-
re præstantibus, percelebris. Deniq, omnium rerum copia, atque opum excellētia
mirabilis. Inuehit in eam totius orbis opes ipse Thamesis, onerarijs nauibus per
sexaginta millia paßuum, ad vrbem præalto alueo nauigabilis

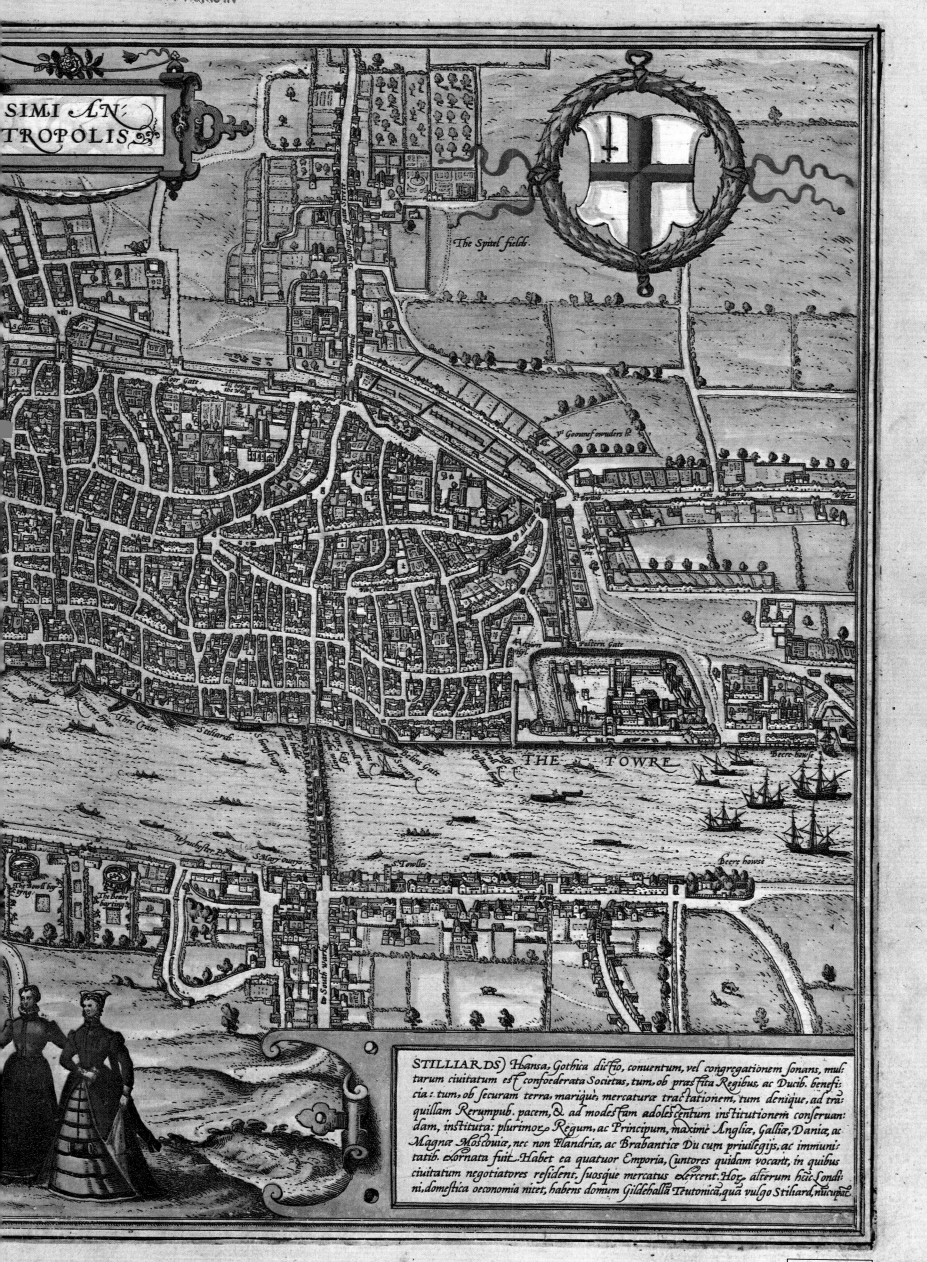

SIMI AN
TROPOLIS

The Spitel fielde.

THE TOWRE

STILLIARDS) Hansa, Gothica dictio, conuentum, vel congregationem sonans, multarum ciuitatum est confoederata Societas, tum ob prasstita Regibus, ac Ducib. beneficia: tum, ob securam terra, marique, mercatura tractationem, tum denique, ad tranquillam Rerumpub. pacem, & ad modestam adolescentum institutionem conseruandam, instituta: plurimor. Regum, ac Principum, maxime Anglia, Gallia, Dania, ac Magna Moscouia, nec non Flandria, ac Brabantice Du cum priuilegijs, ac immunitatib. Exornata fuit. Habet ea quatuor Emporia, Cuntores quidam vocart, in quibus ciuitatum negotiatores resident. suosque mercatus exercent. Hor. alterum hcu Londini, domestica oeconomia nitet, habens domum Gildehalla Teutonica, qua vulgo Stillard, nucupat.

I

LISBO

CASCALE *Lusitaniæ opp:*

A.

OLISIPO, SIVE VT PERVE-
TVSTÆ LAPIDVM INSCRIP-
TIONES HABENT, VLYSIPPO,
VVLGO LISBONA FLORENTIS-
SIMVM PORTVGALLIÆ EMPORIV.

Betheleem

HISPALIS, seuilla Tarapha, Celebre et
peruetustum in Hispania, Bæticæ prouincæ,
emporium, quod Gaditani maris litus amę
niſſimo ſitu illuſtrat. Teeeee

S. Geronimo   S. Laurens   La Puerta de goles   La Caſa de Colon   La Magdalena   St. Paulo

Rio Guadalquir

C

Mar Oceana   Yglesia maior   El Castillo
                              La Culé nueva
Puerta del muro   S. Roque
S. Sebastian   S. Catelina   Athaya

MALAGA

La Torre del Rio   La Yglesia maior

SEVILLA

DIZ

La Punta de S Lucar de barrameda   Rotta
Entrada de la baya
Horno de las françeses
Hospital de la nation flamẽca   Castillo S Philippe   Las Puercas   Srancia de las naos
Tassiques
El Puerto S Maria
Vayonta gorda   Baija de Cadi

CADIZ, olim Gades, eiusdem ho-
minis Insulæ oppidum nobile, por-
tu maris Herculeo freto, templóquè
memoratum.

Camino de Velli

MALACE maritimum, Hispaniæ Bæticæ, oppidum, Malaga deinceps nominatum à Phoenicib. Fran: Tarapha ædi-
ficatum perhibet: Qui anno ante Christi aduentum D. CCC. XXXX ex Asia à mari, quod rubrum vocatur, in
Hispanicum proficiscentes, & hanc incolentes regionem, longinquis continuo nauigationib. incubuerunt, à quibus plereque
ciuitates constructæ leguntur, inter quas Malacæ Ciuitas, in Bætica prouincia, ab eisdem condita fuit. Quæ nunc Episco-
patui nomen præbet. Et mercaturis, varijsquè opificum generib. claret. In qua fictilia vasa nitidissima, conficiuntur &c.

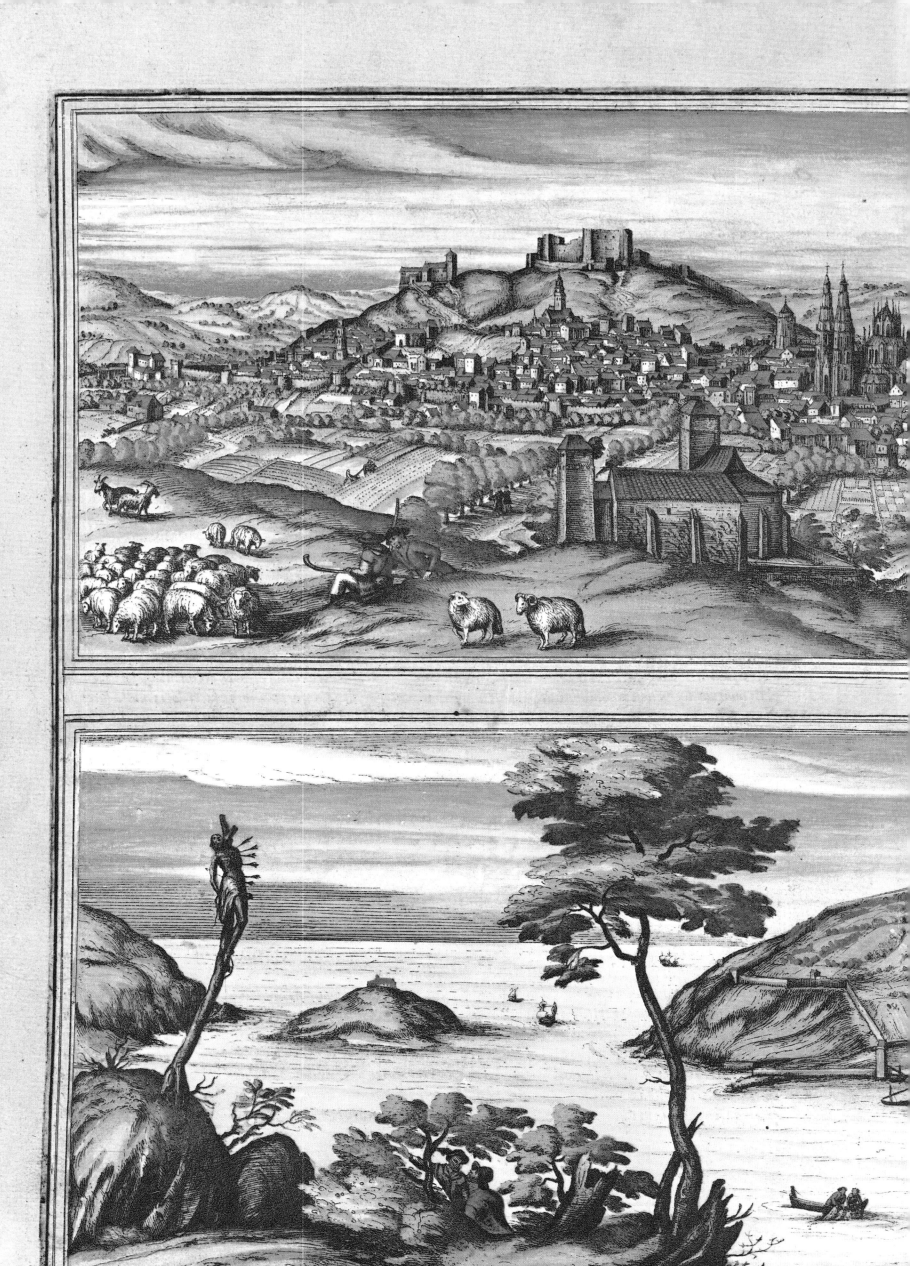

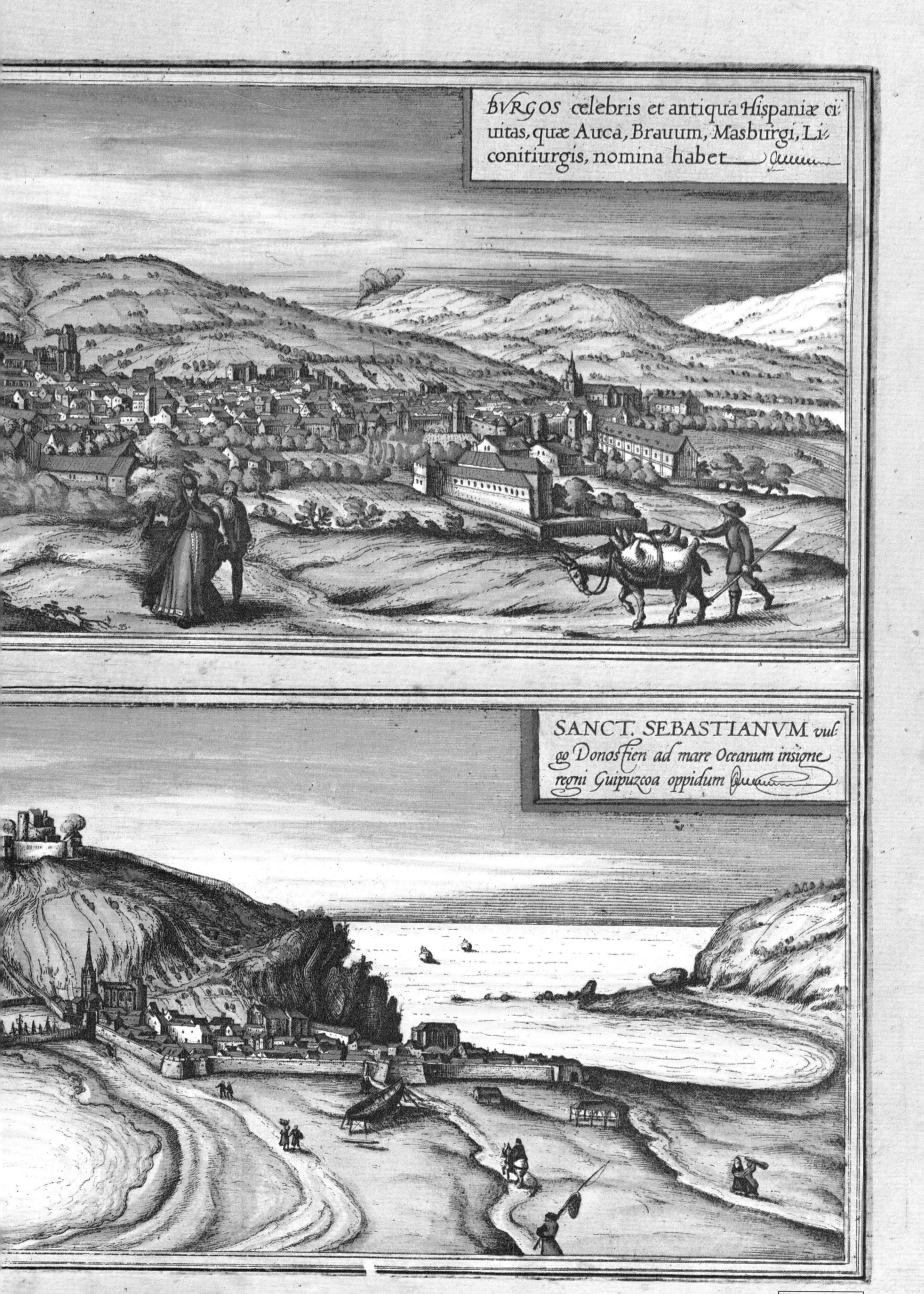

BVRGOS celebris et antiqua Hispaniæ ciuitas, quæ Auca, Brauum, Masburgi, Li-
conitiurgis, nomina habet

SANCT. SEBASTIANVM vul-
go Donostien ad mare Oceanum insigne
regni Guipuzcoa oppidum

IV

MONSPESSVLANVS, MONTPELLIER

Saint Denis

Cum Priuilegio.

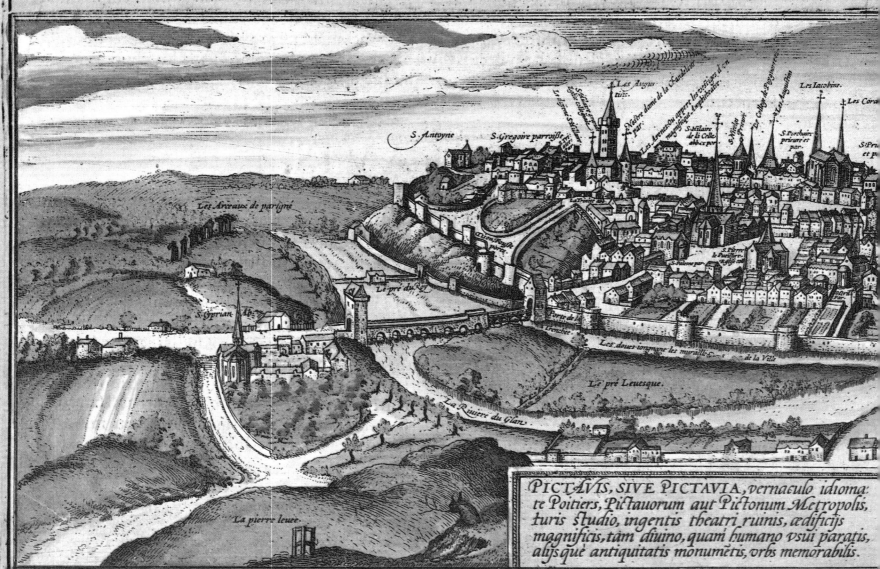

PICTAVIS, SIVE PICTAVIA, vernaculo idioma:
te Poitiers, Pictauorum aut Pictonum Metropolis,
turis studio, ingentis theatri ruinis, ædificijs
magnificis, tàm diuino, quàm humano vsui paratis,
alijsque antiquitatis monumetis, orbs memorabilis.

TVRO, TOVRS.

La Porte de l'esconuerie

A.S.Gratian	E.S.Hilaire.	H.les Cordeliers.
B.S.Martin	F.Le carrefour.	I.Les Iacobins.
C.S.Saturnin	Iehan de Beaune	K.Les Carmes.
D.S.Iulien	G.S.Esteinne.	L.Les Augustins

S.Didier par.
L'orloge
Nostre dame   Le Palais   Nostre dame   A.gealaists
la perte   la grand Egli-   college.
Par.   se et par.   Les Carmes.   S.Cybard par.   Le monstier neuf   L'hostel Dieu des pestiferes.
                                                                S.Germain.   abb. & par.
                                             S.Sauin.   La Porte   Le Chasteau
                                                                S.Ladre.   La porte de
                                                                                                  Rochereul.

Le pré l'Abesse.

La porte du
pont à Ioubert

La Fontaine du   Pont à Ioubert

V

LE ROSNE

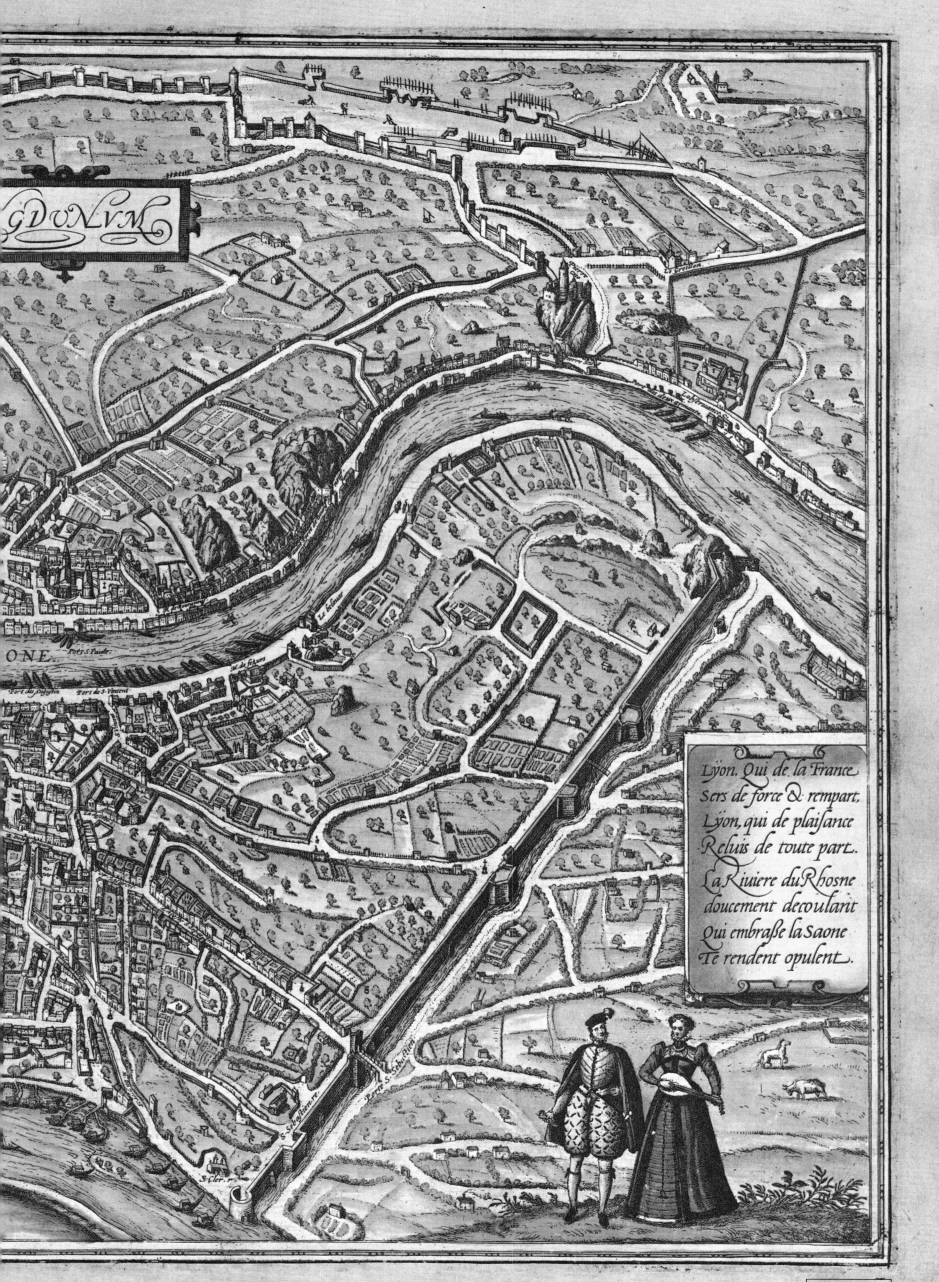

LGDVNVM

ONE

Port. S. Paulr.

Port des Auguftins   Port de S. Vincent

M. de faluers

Le befroar

S. Sebaftienre

Porte S. Sebeftien

S. Clere

Lÿon. Qui de la France
Sers de force & rempart,
Lÿon, qui de plaisance
Reluis de toute part.
La Riuiere du Rhosne
doucement decoulant
Qui embraße la Saone
Te rendent opulent.

ANVERPIA.

PARS FLANDRIAE

SCALDIS FLV.

Les noms des Bou:
leuerts & ra:
pars.
A. Buluardo del Duc.
B. Buluardo de Ernado
C. Buluardo de Toledo
D. Buluardo de Alua
E. Buluardo de Paciotto

Osters hau's. Die Nieuwe Stadt.

ANVERPIA, nobile in Brabantia oppidum, partim maritimum, Gallis, Germanis, Hispanis, Britannis statis frequentata, mercimonijs mirum in modum floret. Sumptuosis tam publicis, quam priuatis ædificijs nitet, nimis Augustissimo D. Virginis templo, cum turri, ex candido lapide altissima; Guilda Hanseatica, Anglica, ac Portugalensium domo; Monasterio Præmonstratensium, monumento Isabelæ Caroli, Ducis Burgundionum Coniugis, nobili. Anno à Christo nato, CIƆ.IƆ.LXVII, Die V. Nouemb. munitissima Anuerpiensium mœnia, à Cronenburgio, vsq; ad Cæsaream portam diuulsa, soloq; æquata fuere: et Arx vallo cincta, fossa & aqua circundata, quinq; propugnaculis ex viuo saxo munita; construitur, habens in circumferentia inter propugnacula superne eminentes decem et tres formas planas, quas alij Pastillos nuncupant, ad hostium propellendas insultus, fortissimas. Intus, late patentem aream, percommodæ claudunt ædes, quas præsidiarij milites incolunt. In areæ medio, statua ænea deaurata, maximis sumtib. fusa Serenissimi Hispaniæ Regis iussu, Illustriss. Duci Albano (cuius vniuersi corporis faciem apprimè refert) beneuolentiæ et gratitudinis ergo pacificatori habitu, posita est Hanc in colosso pedi inscriptionem habens.
FERDINANDO ALVAREZ A TOLEDO ALBÆ DVC. PHILIPPI. II. HISP. APVD BELGAS PRÆFEC. QVOD EXTINCTA SEDITIONE, REBELLIB. PVLSIS RELIGIONE PROCVRATA, IVSTITIA CVLTA. PROVINCIÆ PACE FIRMARIT REGIS OPTIMI MINISTR. FIDELISS. POSITVM.

VII

BRVGÆ, FL
VRBIVM O

BRVGÆ, *vulgo Brugk, Teuto:*
nicæ Flandriæ vrbs omnium
pulcherrima, nitidißimaqué, publi:
carum siquidem, priuatarumqué
ædium in hâc vrbe splendor et
magnificentia, omnem ratio:
nem, omnem dicendi faculta:
tem superat. Optimam vrbi:
um formam, hoc est, orbicula:
rem, situ obtinet, aquis pro:
bè instructa, duplici fossa
ambitur; florentißimum quõ:
dam emporium fuit.

RICARVM
MENTA.

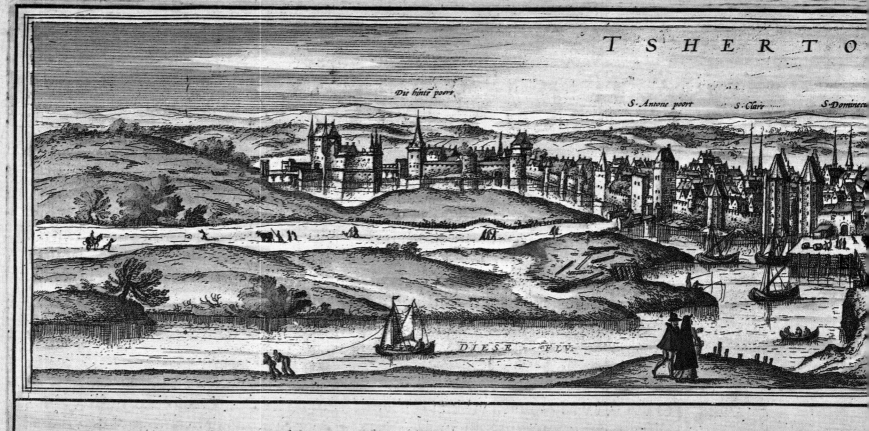

S. Antone poort   S. Clare   S. Domineco

Die hinter poort

DIESE FLV.

L O E

Weernalen   Verloren Coft.   Die Borcht   S. Anst Capp   S. Gertrud   S. Peter

Die Borcht gort   Cloifter onder de Borcht   Vlierbeeck   Linden   Die Dorpstraet porte   S. Marten   S. Cas. Cap.   Stathuis

Porte

De Wyaert poort

LOVANIVM Perantiqua Brabantiæ vrbs, ante Iulij Cæsaris ad uentum in has regiònes, oppidi formam habuit, temporumq̃ succeſsu, in tantam amplitudinem excreuit, nunc vt in ambitu quatuor miliaria Italica colligat. Præstitit hoc Louaniensib. aëris, situsq̃ amœna comoditas. Quos magnificũ etiã D.Petri templũ, ciuiã domᵒ eleganter cõstructa, multoꝝ colle, Vniuersitas, Dela flu, Castrũ à Iulio Cæsare conditũ, multaq̃ admiratione digna, egregie ornant.

M A C

S. Iohan

S. R.

Thof van Hoch straet   S. Peter

Neckerspoel poort   Cayfers hof.

Coepoort.

Borgenstain   Necker spoel

Nicolaes

GENBOSCH

Minre bruren · Spittal · S.Gertruden · S.Peter · Oriten poort · S.Cornelis · Die Vucht poort

BVSCVMDVCIS oppidum ludo literario, & pugnaci populo nobile. Horum arma superiorib. annis haud semel Geldrij sensere, cum qua gente vario certatum est euentu nostris hominibus. In hac vrbe templum est Deiparæ sacrum, opus visendo apparatu. Hadrianus Barlandus.

EN.

Ab. Perck Clost en porte · Satrosen · Heuren Clost

ELEN.

Rom mens Torren · Minebruts · Onser vrouwen kerck · Die Brussel poort · Degem porte

Bogyn hof · DELE FL.

NITIDISSIMÆ CIVITATIS MECHLINEENSIS IN MEDITVLLIO BRABANTIÆ SITÆ EXACTISSIMA DELINEATIO

GROENINGA, siue vt alij, Gru
ninga, Frisiæ vrbs inclyta,
probeque contra hostiles
insultus munita, metropolitica
dignitate percelebris

S Teÿretÿs poort

S. Walborchs kerck

De Fraters

De bodum

Hoge kerck

Poel poort

Leuerberr

S. Martÿns kerck

S. Gertrujt

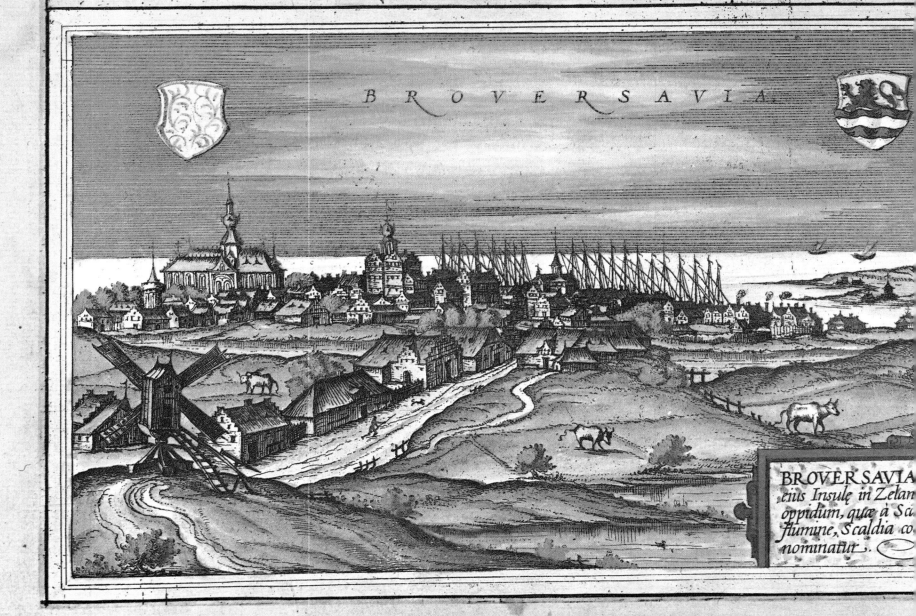

BROVERSAVIA.

BROVERSAVIA
eius Insulę in Zelan
oppidum, quæ à Sa
flumine, Scaldia co
nominatur.

INGA.

Der Heeren huis.
Geestelijcke maechd[s]
...inge poort
Jacopinen
Bottringe poort
S. Martinus
Minores porte.
Vnser lieuer Vr. rouen kercke
S. Iacops gasthuys
Ooster poort
Groot Adwortein Clost.

GORICVM

GORICVM, NO
BILE FLANDRI
Æ OPPIDVM.

DRES

Wind mulen   Pfar Kirchen   Unser lieben Frawen   Daß Schlos

Zeug hauß.

Schieshaus   Muntzhaus

LEI   LIPSIA
RVM S
MERCA
BRE MI

Das Schlos   S. Thomas   Korn hauß

Roßmarck

DEN.

DRESA FLORENTIS
SIMVM MISNIÆ OPP.
ILLVST: SAXONIAE
DVCVM SEDES

Alte Dreszden.

Zollhaus.

Die Elbe.

TTERA:
DIIS ET
RA CELE:
OPPIDVM.

BZIGK

Paulr Kloster.   S. Nicolas   Vniuersiter

Grimeis Thor.

XI

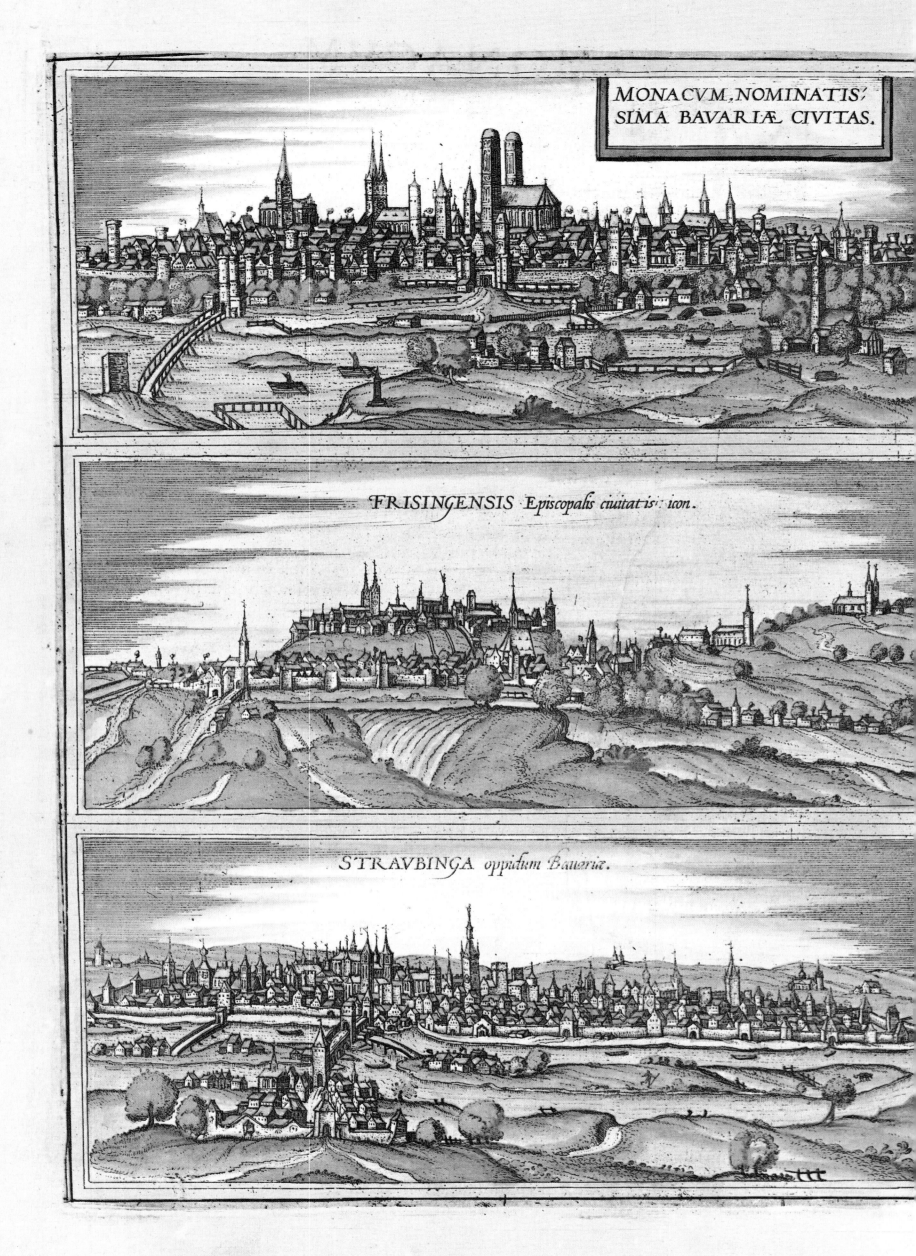

MONACVM, NOMINATIS-
SIMA BAVARIÆ CIVITAS.

FRISINGENSIS Episcopalis ciuitatis icon.

STRAVBINGA oppidum Bauariæ.

NORDLINGA Ciuitas imperialis sita in
Rhetia inferiori transdanubiana, vulgo,
Rieß dicta.

RATISPONA antiquaßima Bauariæ
vrbs, Danubij ripis adiacet.

XII

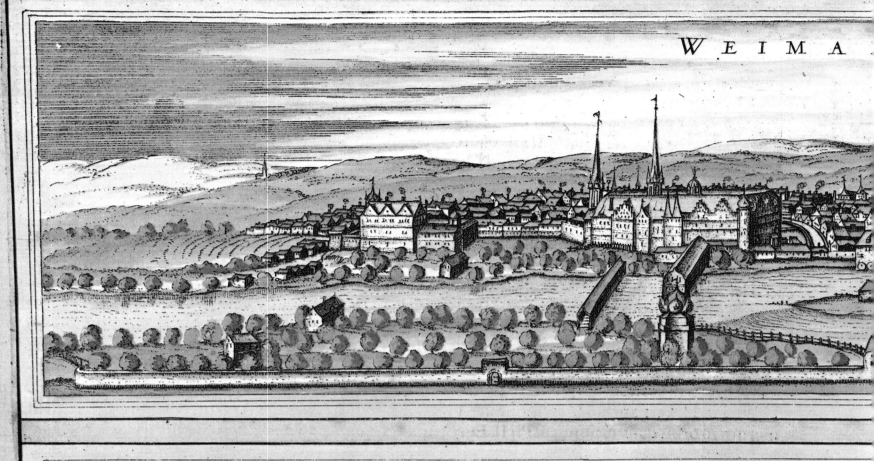

WEIMA

IENA *Thuringiæ vrbs. cum propter Musas, tum vineta clara et celebris.*

GOTHA.

GOTHA, *percelebri muror. ambitu
pugnaculis, formis planis, et arce, omniu
missimu Thuringiæ oppidum. Eius castru
à Sacro Romano Imperio proscriptis, lat
fuit, funditus euersum es*

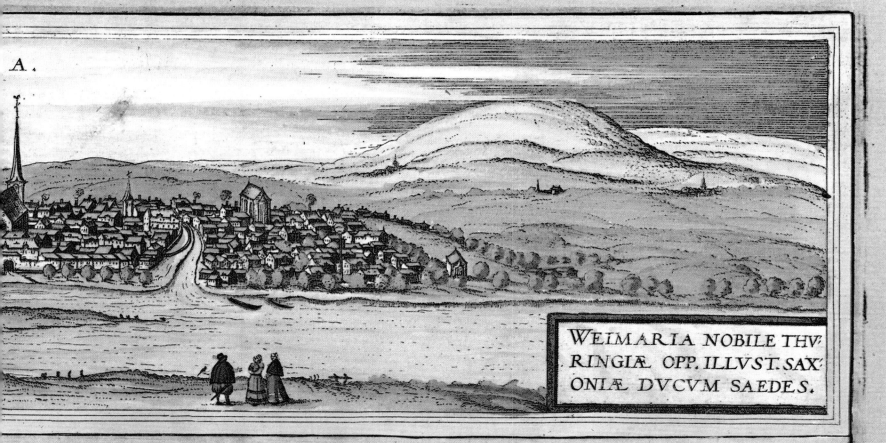

WEIMARIA NOBILE THV-
RINGIÆ OPP. ILLVST. SAX-
ONIÆ DVCVM SAEDES.

ERDFORDIA, *magnifica atq;*
celeberrima Thuringorum vrbs.

Cum privilegio.

FVLDENSIS CIVITATIS, & *celeberrimæ*
abbatiæ eiusdem imago.

S. Andreas.

S. Peter.

S. Katarina.

De Dom.

Tom broderen

S. Iorgen

S. Bartolomeus

LVNEBVRGVM, NOBILIS
SAXONIÆ VRBS, SALINIS
CELEBERRIMA.

Radt hus

S. Iohannes

Des Hertogen

Dat bardewikhr Dor

S. Claus

Dat Titgel hus

BREMA.

S. Marten

S. Scharris.

Viser lue Fruue

Der Doem

Dat Scharis Dor

S. Steffe Kercke

De Natlen

Op der Tiser

Dat Stefens Dor.

Dat Oster Dor

.Martin. *S.Iocob* *S.Magnus* *S.Michael* *S.Egidij* *S.Ciria.us berg*

De Hilge Geist *S.Lambert* *Springint G.* *Kalck berch* *S.Michael.* *S.Siliack*

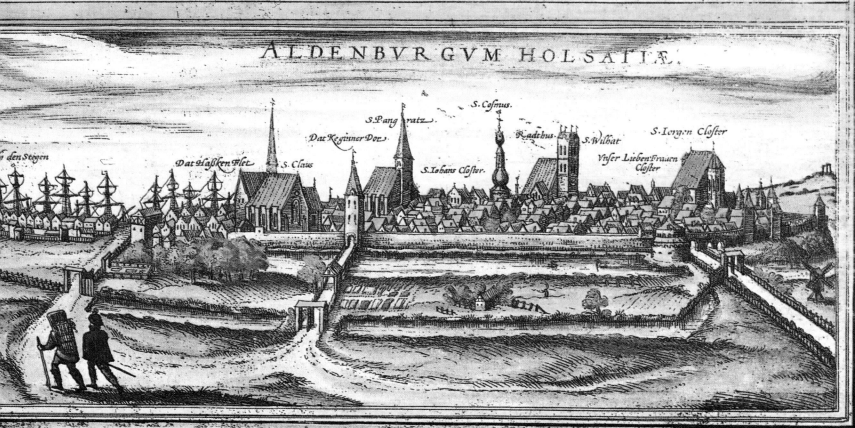

ALDENBVRGVM HOLSATIÆ.

den Stegen *Dat Haßken Flet* *S.Claus* *S.Pangratz.* *Dat Kegiiner Dor.* *S.Cofmus.* *S.Iohans Clofter.* *Radthus* *S.Wilhat* *S.Iergen Clofter* *Vnfer Lieben Frauen Clofter*

XIV

S. Niclaus

MAGDEBVRGVM,
A VENERE QVÆ
HIC QVONDAM COLE
BATVR PARTHENO
POLIS DICTA, metropo-
litica Saxoniæ vrbis, opibus &
authoritate memorabilis, perau-
gusto murorum ambitu, & Al-
bis fluuij viciuitate,
illustris &c.

GVM.

S. Nicol Der Dom.

XV

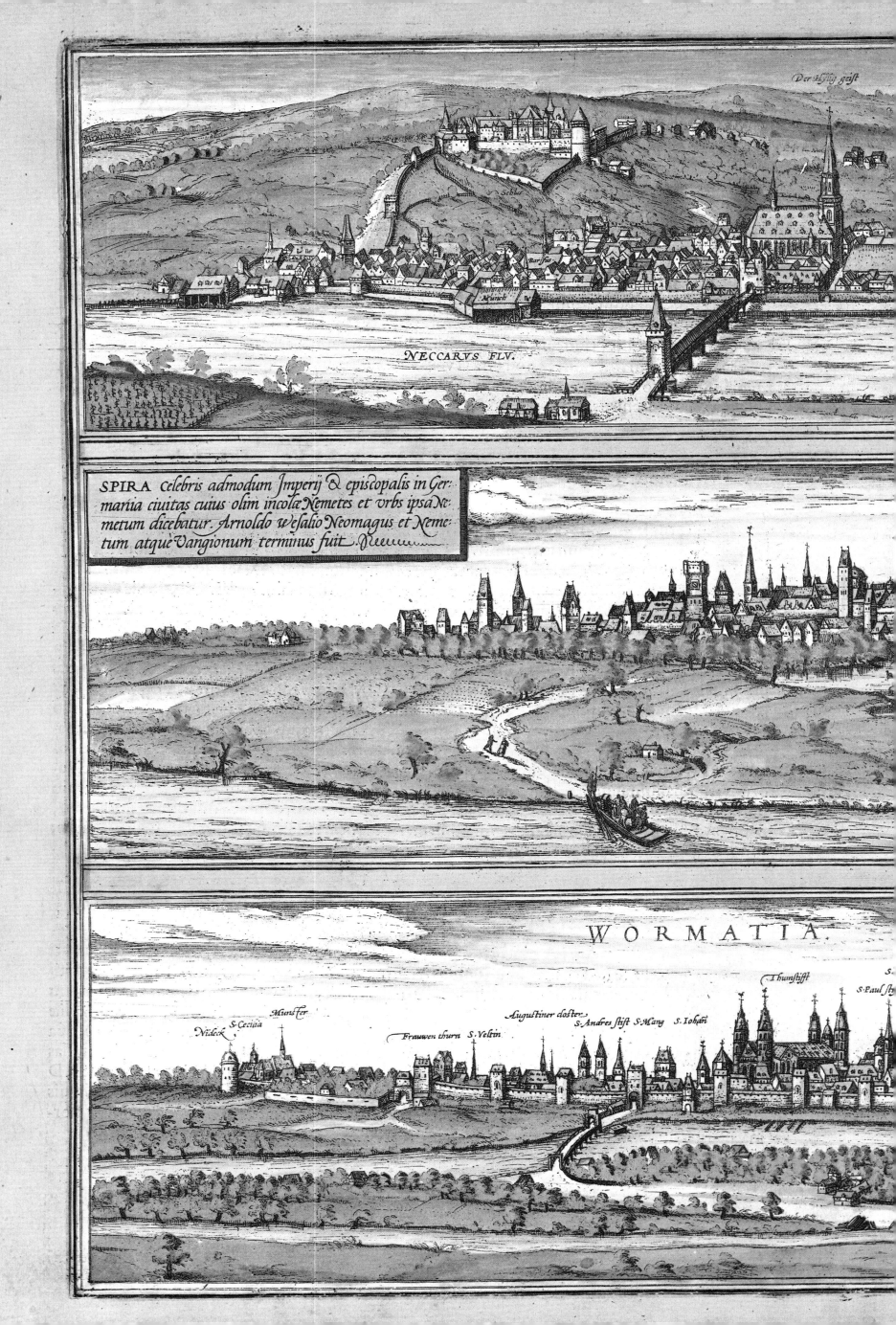

Der öfftig gast

NECCARVS FLV.

SPIRA celebris admodum Imperij & episcopalis in Germania ciuitas cuius olim incolæ Nemetes et vrbs ipsa Nemetum dicebatur. Arnoldo wesalio Neomagus et Nemetum atque Vangionum terminus fuit.

WORMATIA.

Thumstifft

S:Paul st.

Nideck   S.Cecilia   Munster   Augustiner closter   S.Andres stift S:Mang S.Iohan

Frauwen thurn S.Veltin

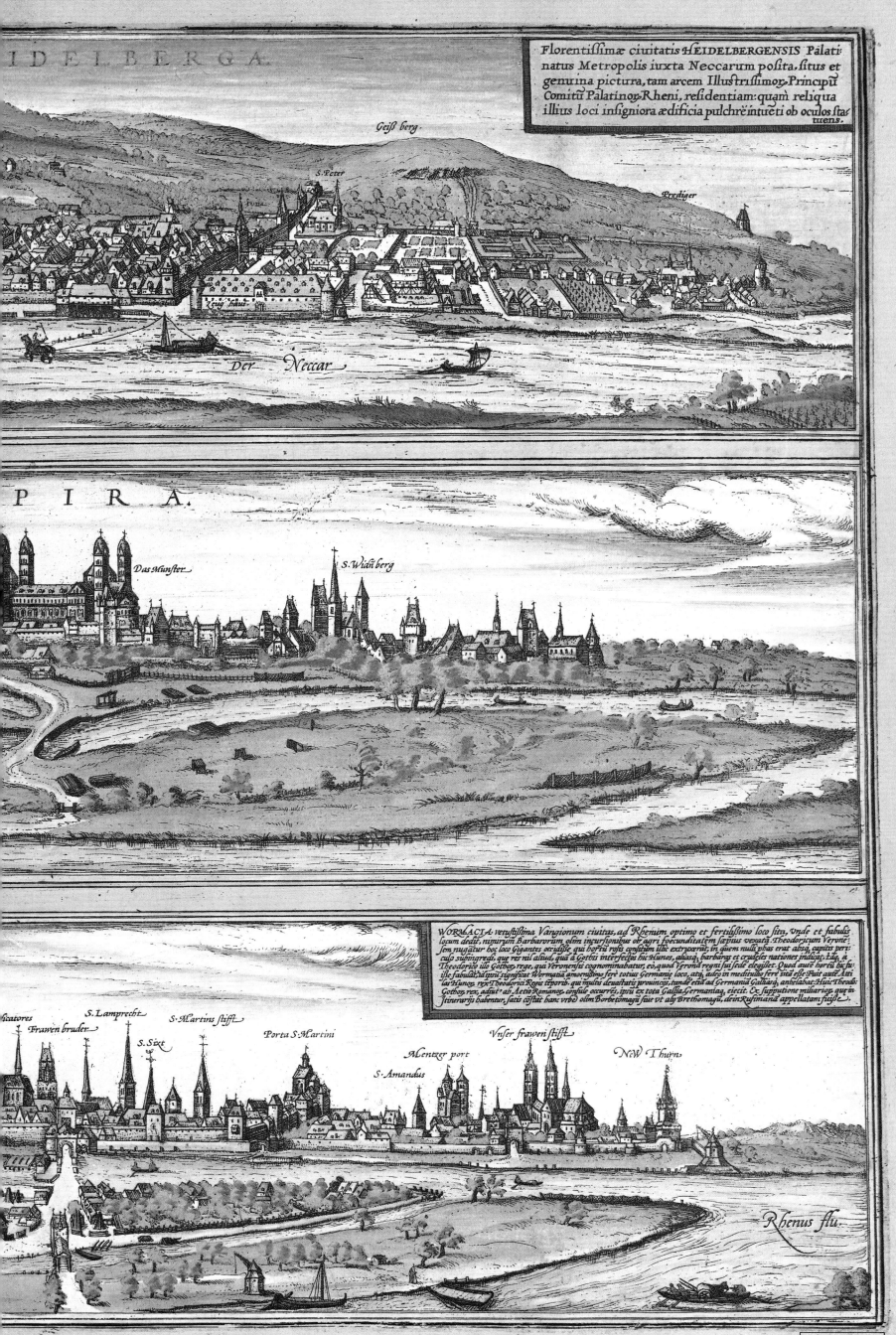

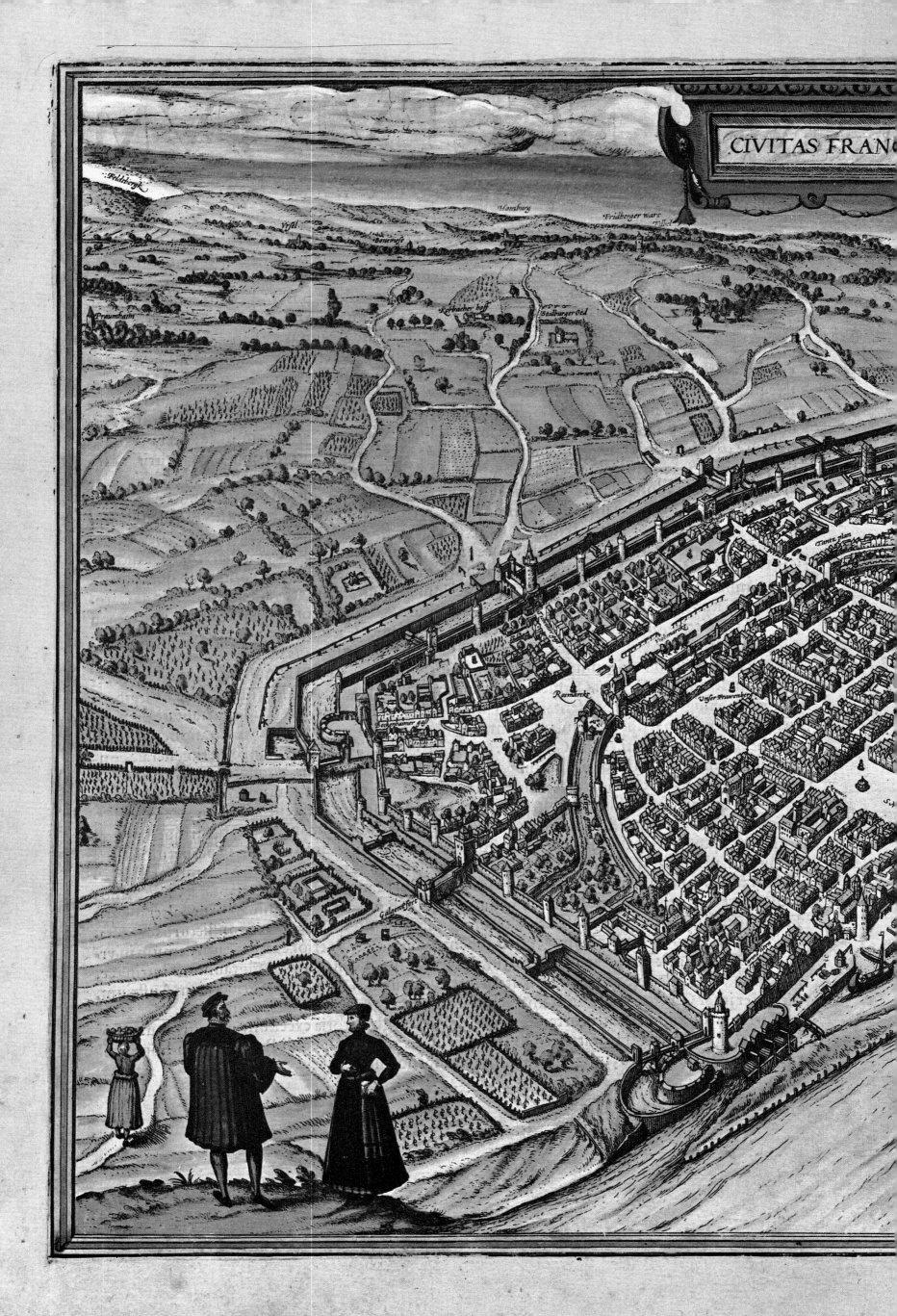

CIVITAS FRANC

Feldbergk

Homburg

Vrsel

Fridberger wart

Bonemese

Praunhaim

Korbacher hoff

Stalburger Oel

Tantz plan

Rosmarckt

Unser Frauenberg

Bockenheimer fass

Galgenefort

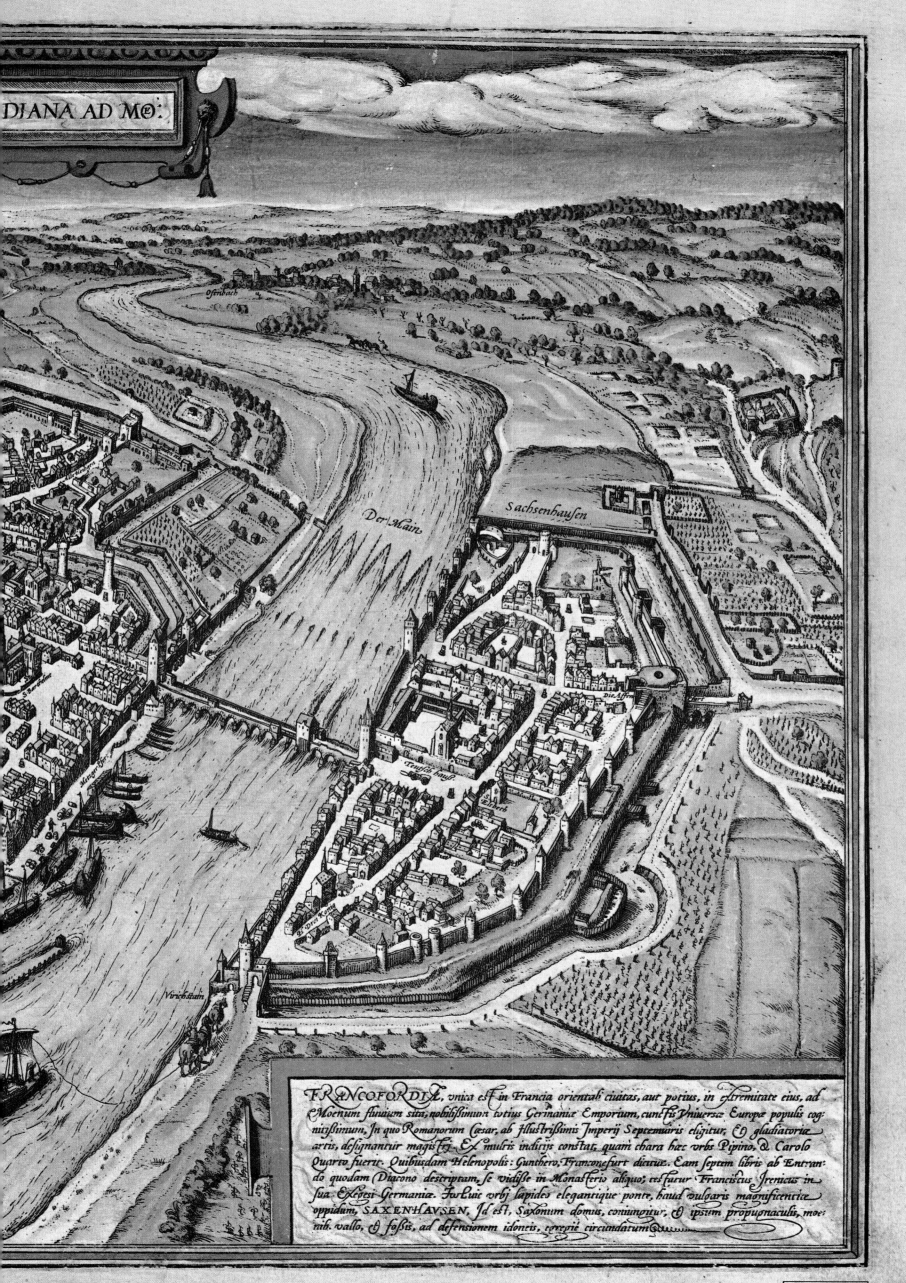

Osenbach

Der Main

Sachsenhausen

Die Affen

Tentsch hauß

S. Berti

S. Berti

Berggr. Thor

Die Drei Konig

Mingerth.

Virich Stain

FRANCOFORDIÆ, vnica est in Francia orientali ciuitas, aut potius, in extremitate eius, ad
Moenum fluuium sita, nobilissimum totius Germaniæ Emporium, cunctis Vniuersæ Europæ populis cog:
nitissimum, In quo Romanorum Cæsar, ab illustrissimis Imperij Septemuiris eligitur, & gladiatoriæ
artis, designantur magistri. Et multis indicijs constat, quam chara hæc orbs Pipino, & Carolo
Quarto fuerit. Quibusdam Helenopolis: Gunthero, Franconefurt dicitur. Eam septem libris ab Entzan:
do quodam Diacono descriptam, se vidisse in Monasterio aliquo, testatur Franciscus Irenicus in
sua Exegesi Germaniæ. Iuzhuic orbi lapides elegantique ponte, haud vulgaris magnificentiæ
oppidum, SAXENHAVSEN, Id est, Saxonum domus, coniungitur, & ipsum propugnaculis, moe:
nib. vallo, & fossis, ad defensionem idoneis, egregie circundatum.

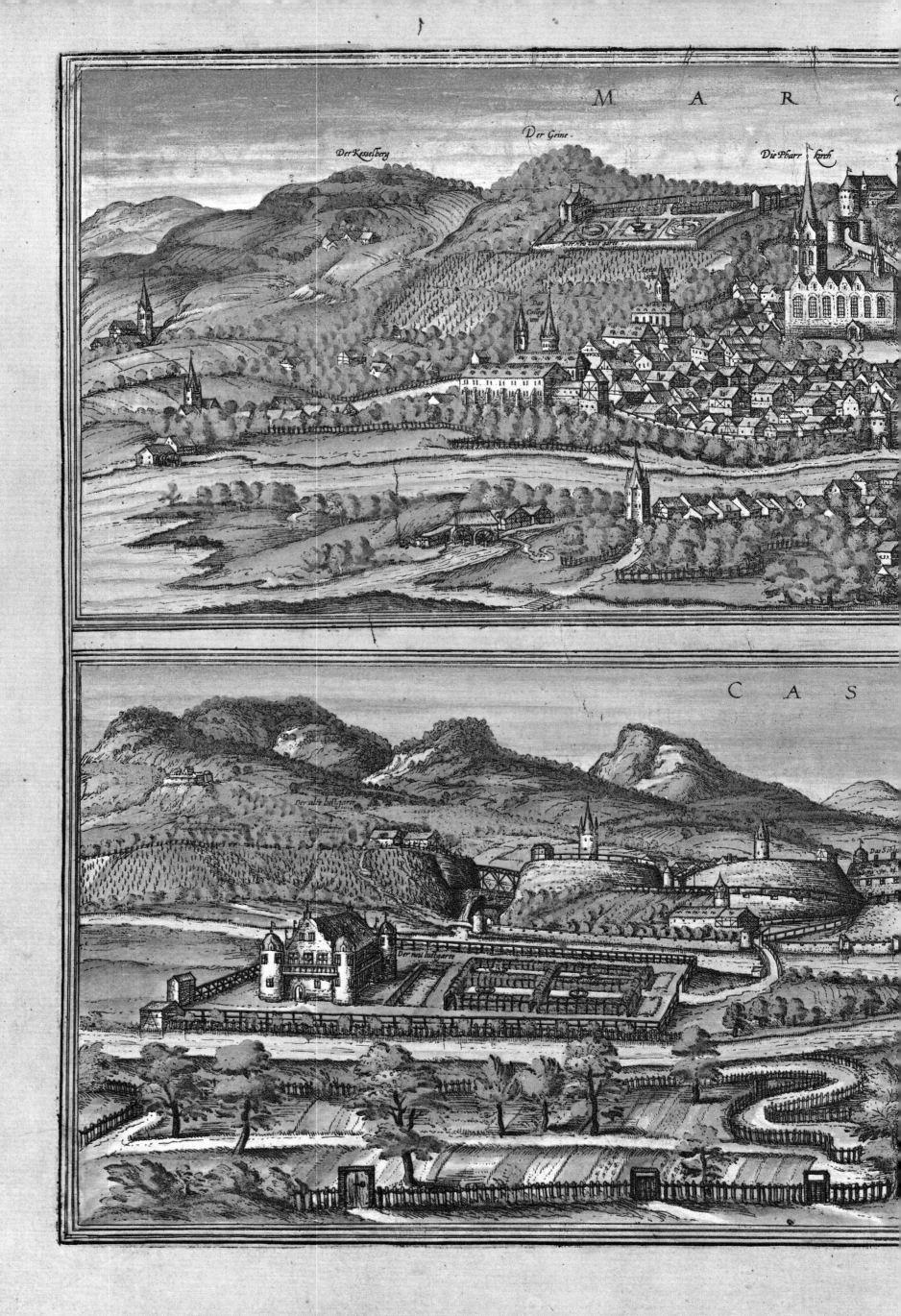

MAR

Der Kesselberg   Der Geine.   Die Pharr kirch

Das Colleg um

CAS

Der alte lustgartn   Der Geine.   Das Schl

Der neu lustgartn

schloß. P V R G.

MARTPVRGVM VRBS
HASSIÆ METROPO͛
LIS, VNIVERSITATE CLARA.

CASSVLA, *communiter Caßel, florentißimũ*
lanigeræ Haßiæ oppidum, aquis, arce, &
propugnaculis fortiter inſtructum, Ptolemęo
Stereontium dicitur.

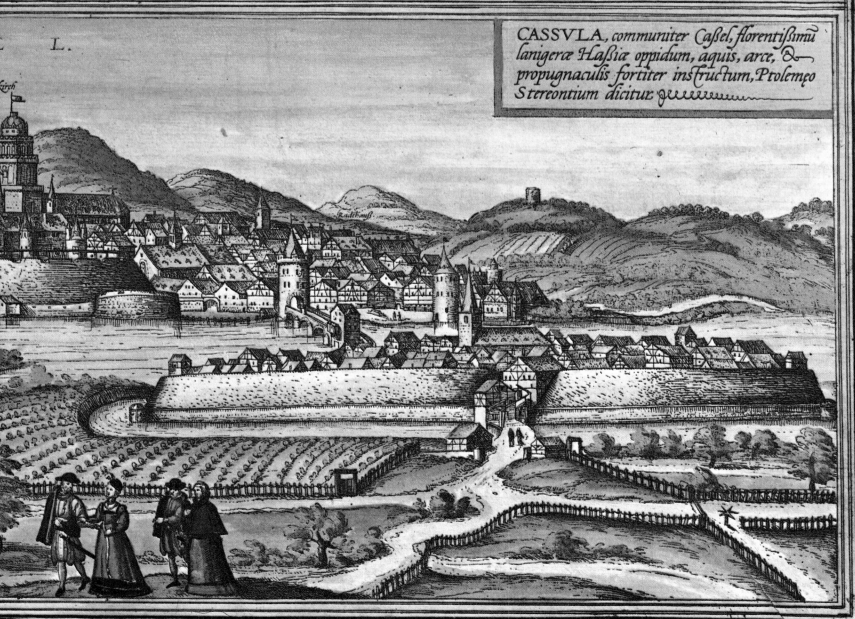

XVIII

WITTENBVRGA

Saxoniæ oppidum, Vniuersali litteroru studio celebre.

WISMARIA, *natura loci populi frequentia, & ædificijs in*
Ducatu Megapolensj, nobile Oppidum

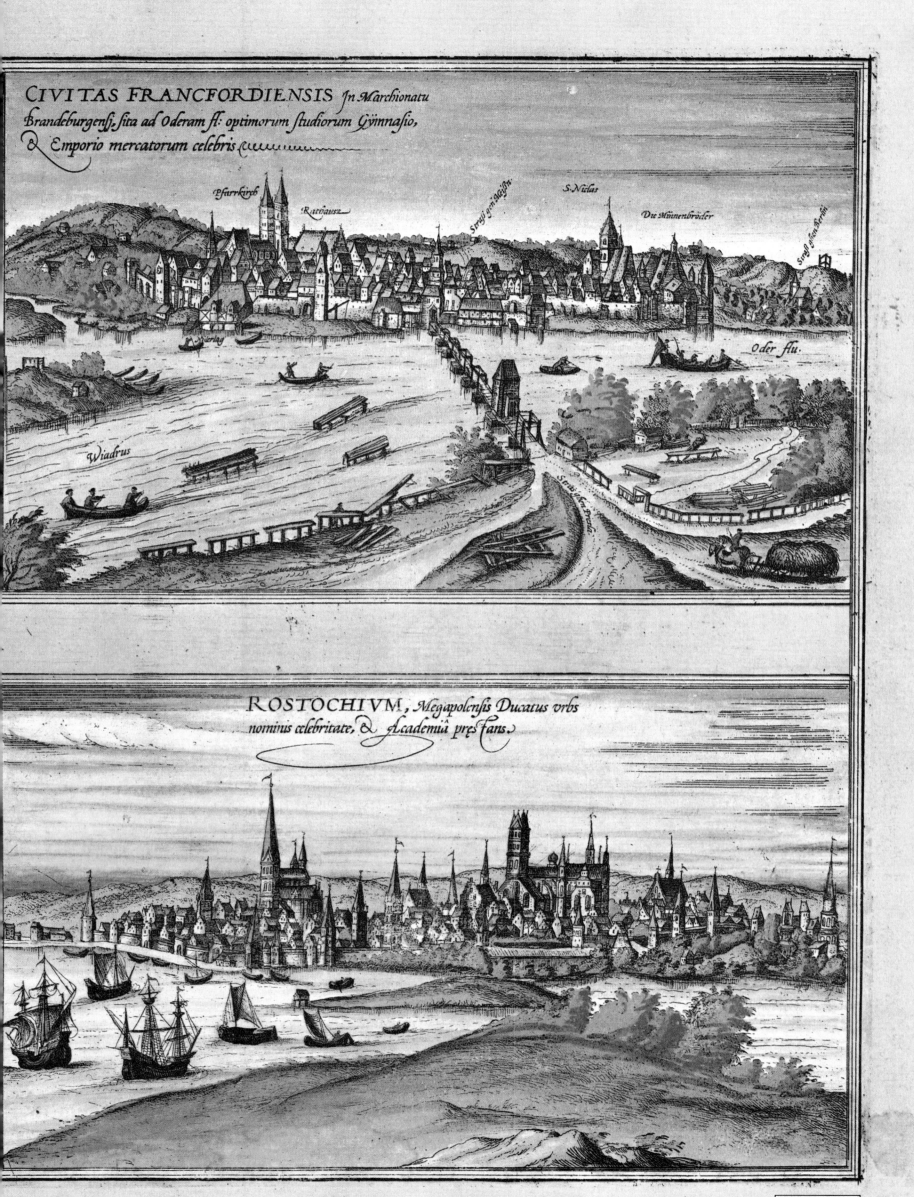

CIVITAS FRANCFORDIENSIS *In Marchionatu Brandeburgensi, sita ad Oderam fl: optimorum studiorum Gÿmnasio, & Emporio mercatorum celebris.*

Pfarrkirch   Rathausz   S. Niclas   Die Münnenbröder

Strefs gen Meiszn   Strefs gen Berlin

Oder flu.

Wiadrus

ROSTOCHIVM, *Megapolensis Ducatus vrbs nominis celebritate, & Academiâ præstans.*

XIX

AVGVS...TA IVXTA

1 Rot thor	21 S.Vrsula kloßt	45 Der Fugger ha.	75 Spittelhof.	106 Hirschengrab.
2 Greßinger th.	22 S.Kathrina klo.	46 Dz dantzhauß.	76 Am Eser.	108 Lang gaß.
3 Einlaß	23 S.Anna kloßt.	47 Eicht hauß.	77 Ritzen marckt.	110 Fischergäßlin.
4 Klencker th.	24 S.Steffans kl.	48 Kornschrand.	78 Weingaß.	111 Rautzigäßlin.
5 Gsundbrunn	25 Parfusser kloßt.	49 Stat Cantzley.	79 Zwerchgaß.	113 Steffani platz.
6 Wertachbruck	26 Hail. ‡ kloßter.	50 Burger stuben.	80 Kirchgaß.	114 Pulvergaß.
7 Fischer th.	27 S.Jorgen kloßt.	51 Kaufleut sstub.	81 Beckengaß.	115 Genßbuhel
8 Luginßland.	28 S.Otmars kirch	52 Rathauß.	82 S.Affra gaß.	116 Lauterlech.
9 Stessinger th.	29 S.Vejts kirch	55 Die Metzg.	83 Am Schwal.	117 Hasen gäßlin
10 Olblater th.	30 S.Johañ kirch	57 Pfrundhauß.	85 Clesattels gaß.	118 S.Iaco. gart
11 Jacober thor	31 S.Gilgen kirch	58 Schlachthauß.	86 Schonawrgaß.	119 Rosen gaßlin
12 Vogel thor	32 Vnser frawen ki.	64 Katzenstadel.	89 Findelhauß.	120 Rapperzipfel.
13 Schwiboger th.	33 Jacober kirch.	65 Ob dem Creütz	92 Am Judenberg.	122 Prielbruck
14 H. Creütz th	34 Das Spittal.	66 Zeughauß.	94 Berlerg.	124 Rosmarckt
15 Onser frawē th	35 S.Peters kirch.	67 Juden kirchof.	97 Staingaß.	125 Ober newgang
16 Parfusser th.	36 Stern kloster.	68 Kornhauß.	99 Opsmarckt.	126 Mittel gang
17 S Virichs kloßt	37 Raassamer hof.	70 Kalck hütt.	100 S.Johans gaß.	127 Vndter gang
18 Prediger kloß	38 Saltz stadel.	71 Blaterhauß.	101 Schmidgaß.	130 Sachßen gaß.
19 S.Moritzē kir.	39 Wein stadel.	72 Die Fuggerej	104 Fronhof.	131 Meiting gaß.
20 H. Grab.	40 Sigelhauß.	73 Zur sackpfeiffn	105 Die Pfaltz.	133 Maurberg

HABET DELINE

VAM HIS
ORIBVS.

Augustam Vindelicor, celeberrimam, et peruetustam, Superioris Germaniæ vrbem, post funestam, varianam cladem, subactis Vandalicis, Octauianus Aug. expugnat, restaurat, auget, & tribus Romanor. millib. habitandam tradit, Strabo lib. 4. Hinc Augusta est nomen sortita. Vngari, tum eam inuadut, quibus ab Ottone I. graui prælio fusis, Romano Imperio, restituitur. Sumptuosissimis ædificijs, plateis amplis, ac nitidis, moenijs, aggeribusq; munitissimis, celeberrimis negotiorum commercijs, polytiæ idea, incolis opulentissimis, diligenti pauperum cura, Episcopatu, &c. nobilitatur.

XX

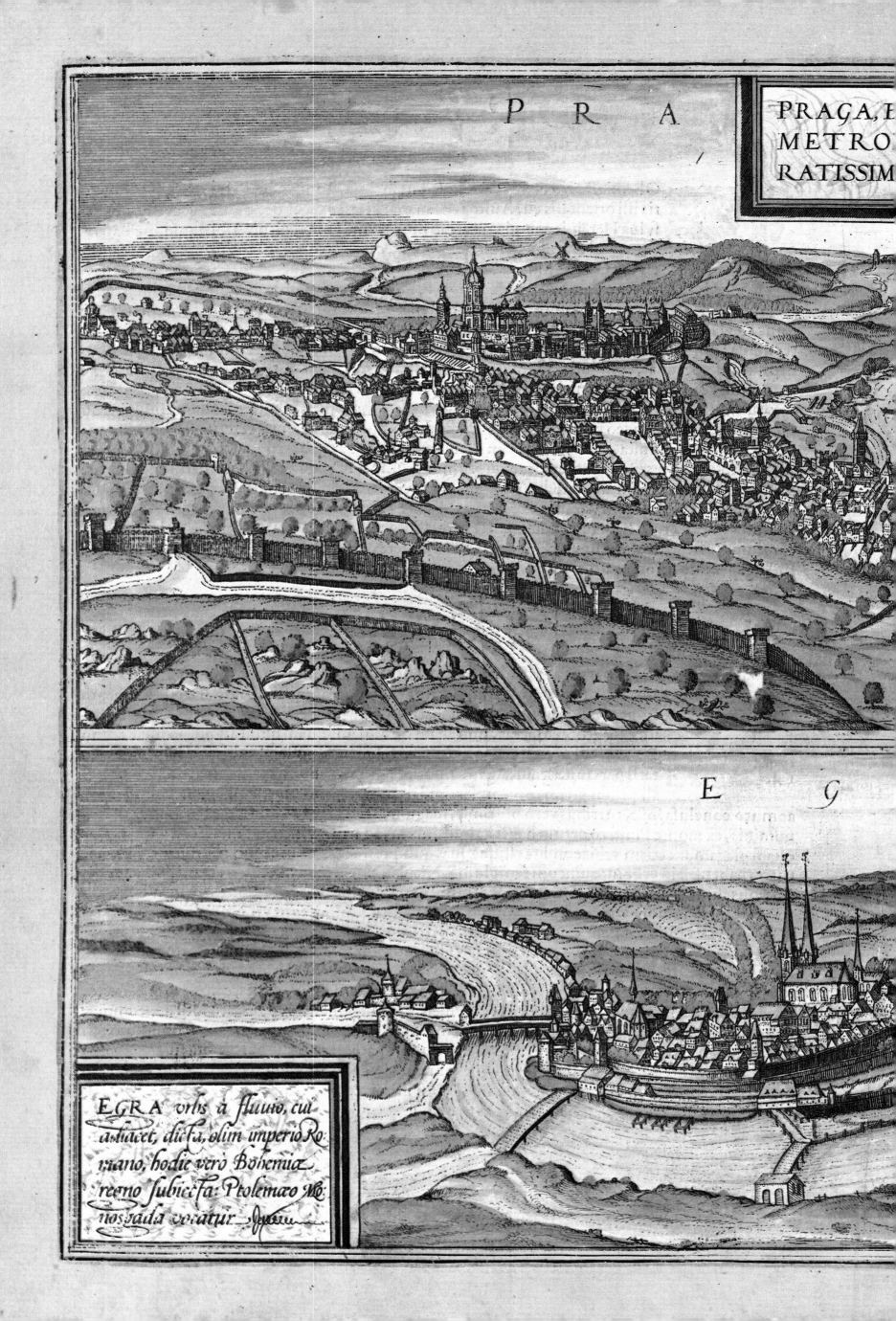

PRA

PRAGA,
METRO
RATISSIM

E G

EGRA vrbs à fluuio, cui
adiacet, dicta, olim imperio Ro:
mano, hodie vero Bohemiæ
regno subiecta: Ptolemæo Me:
nos gada vocatur.

G A.

A.

MIAE
ACCV
RESSA.

XXI

SVICIA *Schwytz*

Ad foederis focietatem recipitur,
Anno Salutis, M. CCC. XV.

SYLVANIA *Vnderwalden*

M. CCC. XV.

VGIVM

M. CC

TYGVRVM   M. CCC. LI.   *Zurich.*

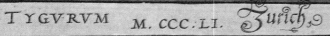

CIVITAS VRSINA   M. CCC. LIII.   *Bern.*

FRIBVRGVM   M. CCCC. LXXXI.   *Fryburg.*

CIVITAS SOLOTVRENSIS.   *Solothurn.*
M. CCCC. LXXXI.

EDERATORVM HELVETIAE.

GLARONA Glaris
M. CCC. LII.

BASILEA Basell
M. D. I.

LVCERNA M. CCC. XXXII. Lucern

VRSELLA M. CCC. XV. Vri

SCHAPHVSIA M. D. I. Schaffhusen

APPENCELLA M. D. XIII. Appenzell

XXII

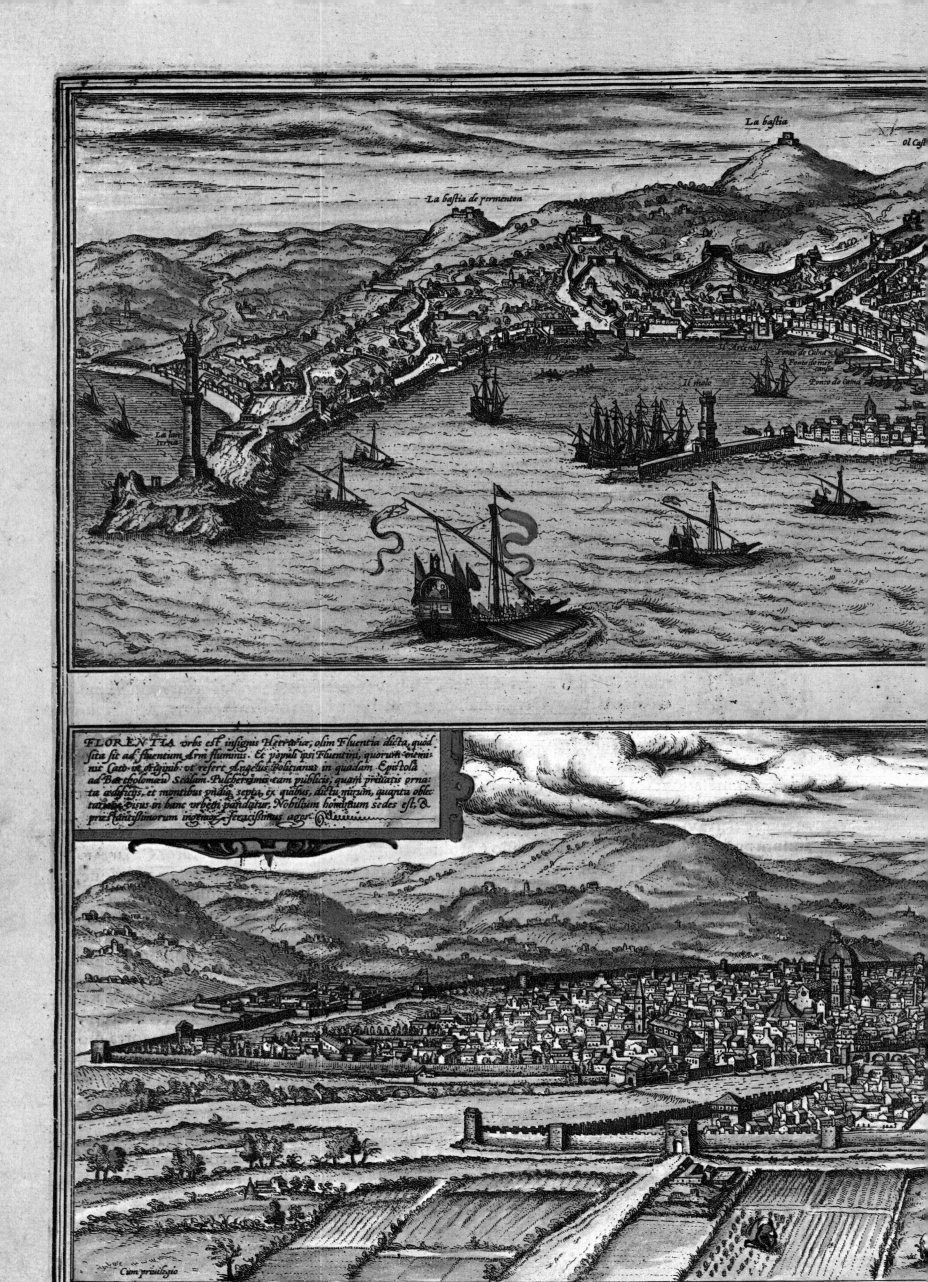

La bastia

ol Cast

La bastia de formenton

Il Arsenal

Ponto de Calva

Ponto de mez

Il molo

Ponto do Calva

La lanterna

FLORENTIA orbs est insignis Hetruriæ, olim Fluentia dicta, quòd sita sit ad fluentum Arni fluminis. Et populi ipsi Fluentini, quorum meminit Cato & Plinius: ut refert Angelus Politianus in quadam Epistola ad Bartholomæum Scalam. Pulcherrima tam publicis, quàm privatis orna ta ædificiis, et montibus undiq; septa, ex quibus, dictu mirùm, quanta oblectatio & visus in hanc urbem panditur. Nobilium hominum sedes est, & præstantissimorum ingenia, feracissimus ager.

Cum privilegio

GENVA.

La forca   S.Bertholome darm   Consolation   N'ra dona del monte: Besangno

Vielle

Nra dona de gratia   L.G.Conte   Ale.fand

FLORENTIA

XXIII

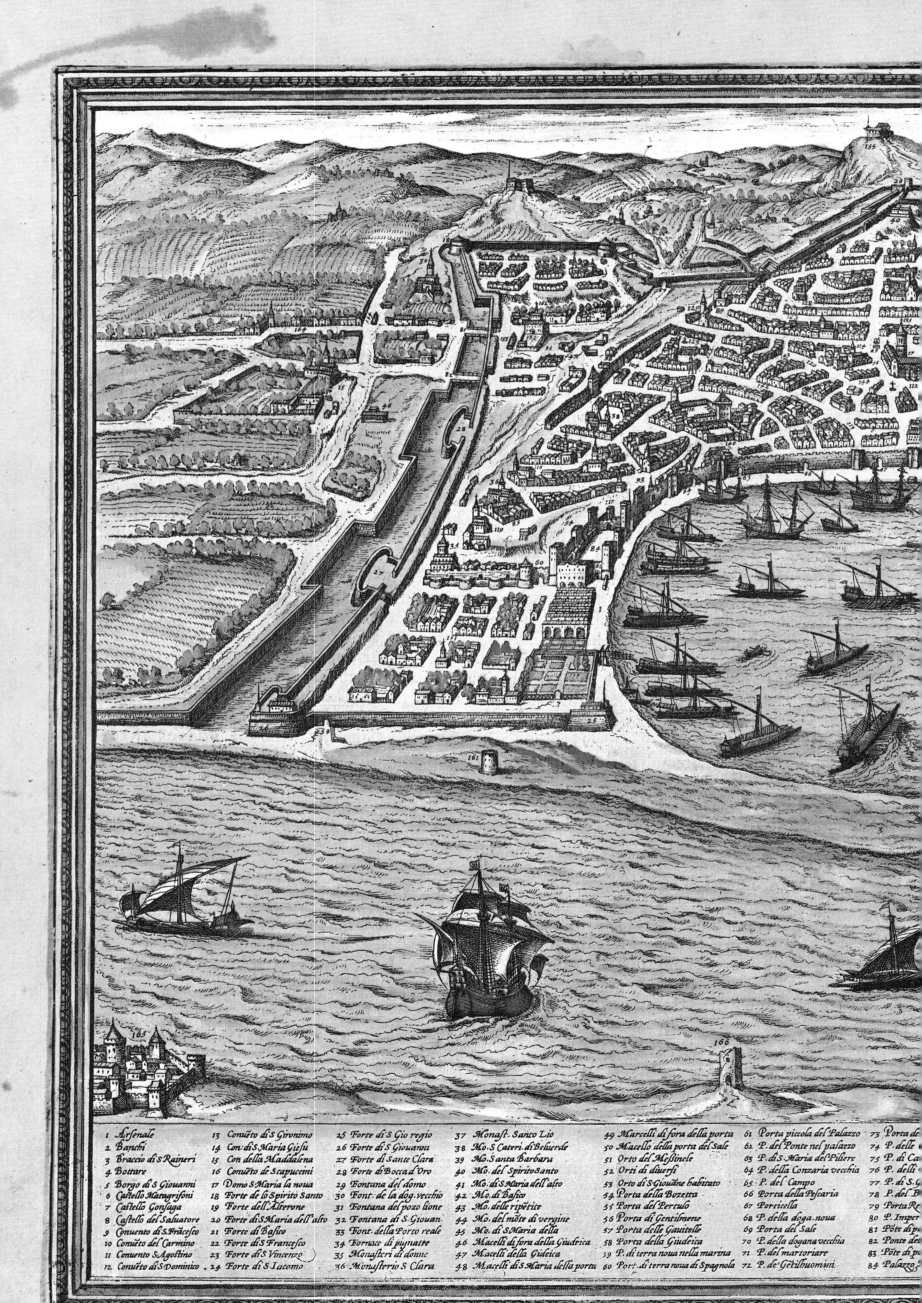

1 Arsenale	13 Conuēto di S Gironimo	25 Forte di S Gio regio	37 Monast. Santo Lio	49 Marcelli di fora della porta	61 Porta piccola del Palazzo	73 Porta de
2 Banchi	14 Con: di S Maria Giesu	26 Forte di S Giouanni	38 Mo. S Caterī. di Behuerde	50 Macello della porta del Sale	62 P. del Ponte nel palazzo	74 P. delle
3 Braccio di S Raineri	15 Con della Maddalena	27 Forte di Sante Clara	39 Mo. S anta Barbara	51 Orto del Mestinele	63 P. di S Maria del Piliere	75 P. di Ca
4 Bottare	16 Comūto de Scapuccini	28 Forte di Bocca d'Oro	40 Mo. del Spirito Santo	52 Orti di diuersi	64 P. della Conzaria vecchia	76 P. delli
5 Borgo di S Giouani	17 Domo S Maria la noua	29 Fontana del domo	41 Mo. di S Maria dell'alto	53 Orto di S Giouāne habitato	65 P. del Campo	77 P. G
6 Castello Matagrisoni	18 Forte de lo Spirito Santo	30 Font: de la dog. vecchio	42 Mo. di Basto	54 Porta della Bozetta	66 Porta della Pescaria	78 P. del Re
7 Castello Gonsaga	19 Forte dell'Alterone	31 Fontana del pozo lione	43 Mo. delle ripetite	55 Porta del Pertulo	67 Porticella	79 Porta Re
8 Castello del Saluatore	20 Forte di S Maria dell'alto	32 Fontana di S. Giouan.	44 Mo. del mōte di vergine	56 Porta di Gentilmene	68 P. della doga. noua	80 P. Imper
9 Conuento di S Frācesco	21 Forte di Basto	33 Font. della Porto reale	45 Mo. di S Maria della	57 Porta delle Gantlite	69 Porta del Sale	81 Pōte di
10 Conuēto del Carmino	22 Forte di S Francesco	34 Fornace di pignatte	46 Macelli di fora della Giudrica	58 Porta della Giudeica	70 P. della dogana vecchia	82 Ponte
11 Conuēto S Agostino	23 Forte di S Vincenzo	35 Monasteri di donne	47 Macelli della Gideica	59 P. di terra noua nella marina	71 P. del martoriare	83 Pōte di p
12 Conuēto di S Dominico	24 Forte di S Iacomo	36 Munasterio S Clara	48 Macelli di S Maria della porta	60 Port: di terra noua di Spagnola	72 P. de'Gētilhuomini	84 Palazzo

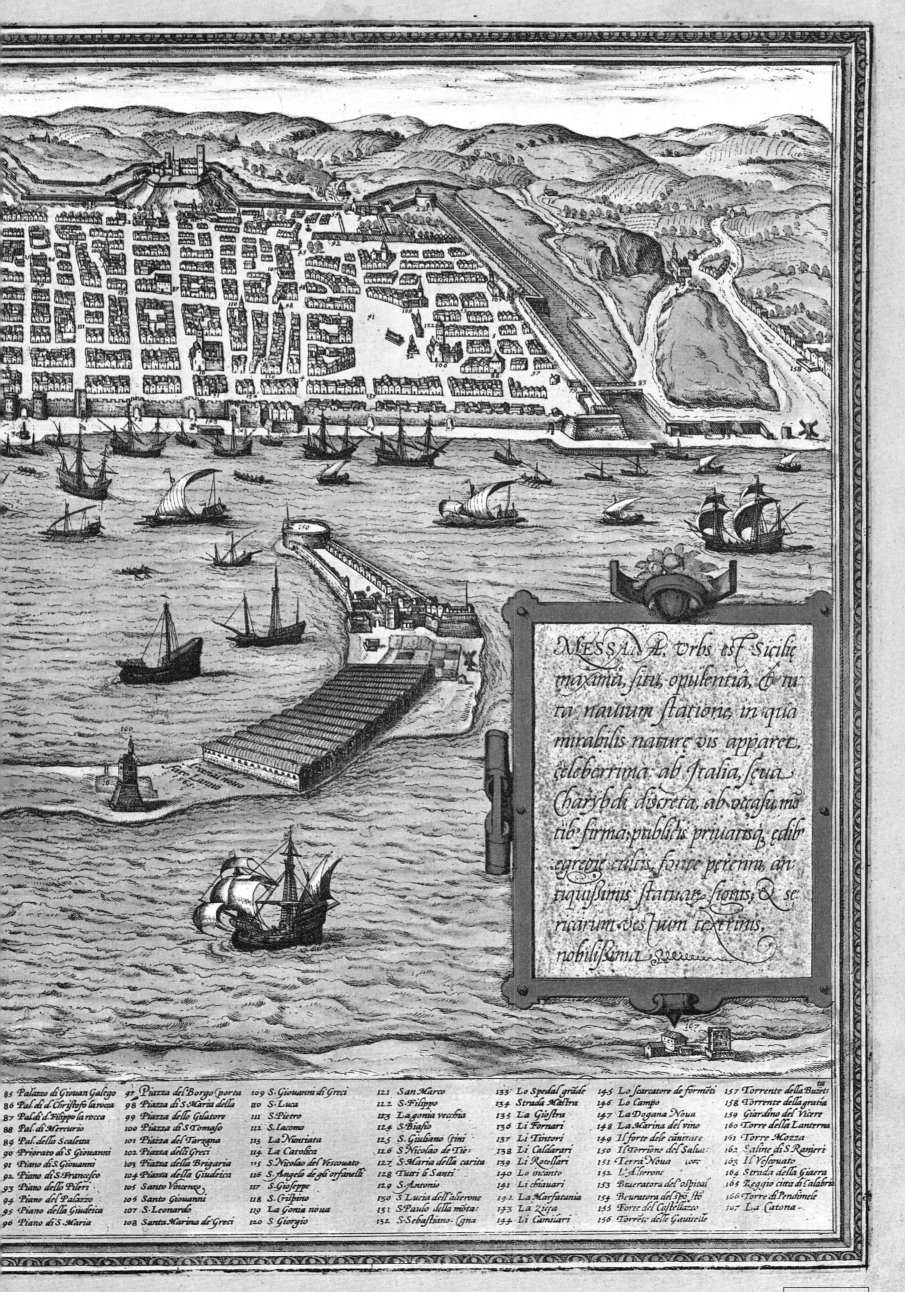

MESSANA, vrbs est Siciliae maxima, situ, opulentia, & tuta navium statione, in qua mirabilis naturae vis apparet, celeberrima: ab Italia, seua Charybdi discreta, ab occasu montib. firma, publicis priuatisq; aedib egregie cultis, fonte perenni, antiquissimis statuae, signis, & sericarum vestium textrinis, nobilissima &c.

MEDIOL

Porta Vercellina

S. Nicolo

Porta Ticinese

Ænd: Alc Des armes
de cesfe Ville
de Milan

L'enfant naisfât d'un Serpent par la bouche
De ton clair Sang les nobles armes touche,
Nous auons veu d'Alexandre Monarque
Pour s'annoblir, monnoÿe à belle marque
Quand fils d'Ammon sous forme Serpétine
Se dict conceu par Semence diuine
On dict Serpens par bouche Serpenter
Nee est Pallas du ceruceau de Jupiter

MEDIOLANVM Metropolis Insubrium, vulgò Mila:
no, vrbs potentiæ & dignitatis eximiæ, quæ ob præstantè
loci commoditatè, Imperatorȝ Romanorum sedes, plerumȝ
fuit, qui superbissimis eam ædificijs exornarûnt. Circa quam
nobilis regio tum coeli temperie, tum soli fertilitate, et afflu:
enti rerum copia, vnde ciuitas suo abundans populo, et pro:
prijs nitens viribus, semper gentis fuit caput, et quotiens
euersa, pos̄t excidium restituta, vbertate agri, et propin:
quitate Alpium, ex quibus hominum copia affluit. Ingè:
ti incremento res Mediolanensis tempore Gratiani Cæsaris
aucta erat. Nè quingentos et amplius annos, neȝ, ab externo hos:
te, nec intestino bello Insubres vexari fuere. Durauit illa foe:
licitas vsȝ ad D. Ambrosij tempora, quib̄ Arriana heresis,
maximis calamitatib̄ hanc vrbè affecit. Deinde Attila in Ita:
liã ingress. Mediolanum diruit. Instauratú, aliquáto tè:
pore quieuit. Mox à Longobardis maximis agitatur moles:
tijs, Quib̄ à Carolo Magno domitis, ãnos trecétos et sexagíta floru:
it. Deide verò Fridericus Barbarossa Mediolanú solo æquauit.
Cuius incole tunde Parmensiũ et Placentinorȝ ope, tanto ani:
mgȝ ardore patriã restaurarût, vt multo quam ante ditior,
potètior, frequentiorȝ, extiterit. Quod sane maximã huius
vrbis potentiã arguit, quod post tam frequètes hostiũ di:
reptiones, in tantã magnitudinem rursus excreuerit.

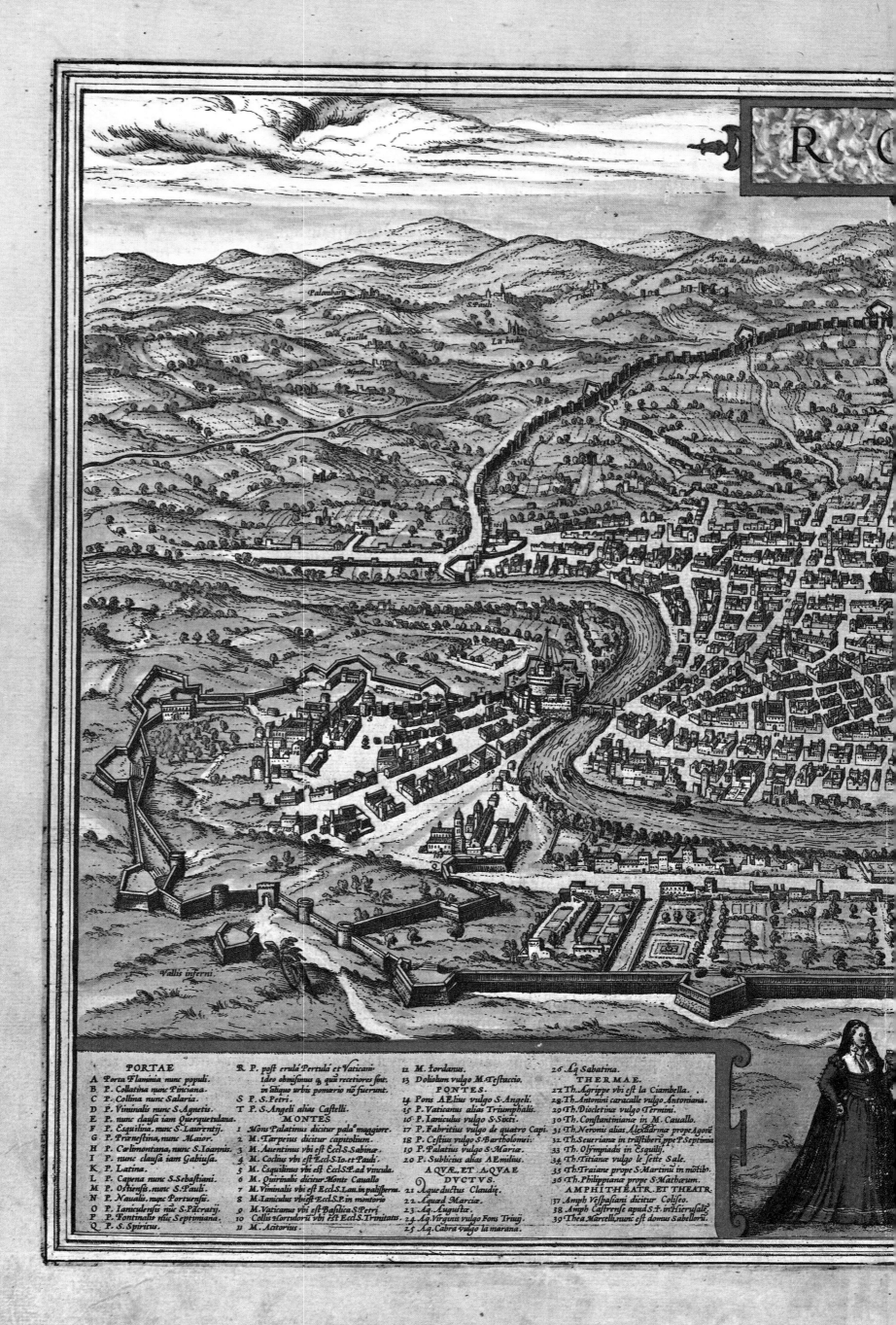

PORTAE

A Porta Flaminia nunc populi.
B P. Collatina nunc Pinciana.
C P. Collina nunc Salaria.
D P. Viminalis nunc S. Agnetis.
E P. nunc clausa iam Querquetulana.
F P. Esquilina, nunc S. Laurentij.
G P. Præneſtina, nunc Maior.
H P. Cælimontana, nunc S. Ioannis.
I P. nunc clausa iam Gabiusa.
K P. Latina.
L P. Capena nunc S. Sebaſtiani.
M P. Oſtienſis. nunc S. Pauli.
N P. Naualis, nunc Portuenſi.
O P. Ianiculenſis nūc S. Pācratij.
P P. Fontinalis nūc Septimiana.
Q P. S. Spiritus.

R P. poſt erulã Pertulã et Vaticanʉ
       ideo obniſſinuʉ q̃, qui recetiores ſint.
       in aliquo urbis pomœrio nõ fuerunt.
S P. S. Petri.
T P. S. Angeli alias Caſtelli.

MONTES

1 Mons Palatinus dicitur pala° maggiore.
2 M. Tarpeius dicitur capitolium.
3 M. Auentinus vbi eſt Eccl. S. Sabinæ.
4 M. Cœlius vbi eſt Eccl. S. Io. et Pauli.
5 M. Esquilinus vbi eſt Eccl. S. P. ad vincula.
6 M. Quirinalis dicitur Monte Cauallo
7 M. Viminalis vbi eſt Eccl. S. Lau. in paliſterm.
8 M. Ianiculus vbi eſt Eccl. S. P. in montorio
9 M. Vaticanus vbi eſt Baſilica S. Petri
10 Collis Hortulorū vbi eſt Eccl. S. Trinitatis.
11 M. Acitorius.

12 M. Iordanus.
13 Doliolum vulgo M. Teſtaccio.

PONTES.

14 Pons AElius vulgo S. Angeli.
15 P. Vaticanus alias Triumphalis.
16 P. Ianiculus vulgo S. Sixti.
17 P. Fabritius vulgo de quatro Capi.
18 P. Ceſtius vulgo S. Bartholomei.
19 P. Palatius vulgo S. Mariæ.
20 P. Sublicius alias AEmilius.

AQVÆ, ET AQVAE DVCTVS.

21 Aque ductus Claudiæ.
22 Aquad Marcia.
23 Aq. Auguſta.
24 Aq. Virginis vulgo Fons Triuij.
25 Aq. Cabra vulgo la marana.

26 Aq. Sabatina.

THERMAE.

27 Th. Agrippe vbi eſt la Ciambella.
28 Th. Antonini caracalle vulgo Antoniana.
29 Th. Diocletinæ vulgo Termini.
30 Th. Conſtantinianæ in M. Cauallo.
31 Th. Neronis alias Alexãdrinæ prope Agonū
32 Th. Seueriana in trãſtiberi, p̃pe P. Septimia
33 Th. Olympiadis in Esquiliis.
34 Th. Titianæ vulgo le ſeite Sale.
35 Th. Traiane prope S. Martinū in mõtib.
36 Th. Philippianæ prope S. Matthæum.

AMPHITHEATR. ET THEATR.

37 Amph. Veſpaſiani dicitur Coliſeo.
38 Amph. Caſtrenſe apud S. †. in Hierusalē.
39 Thea. Marcelli, nunc eſt domus Sabellorū.

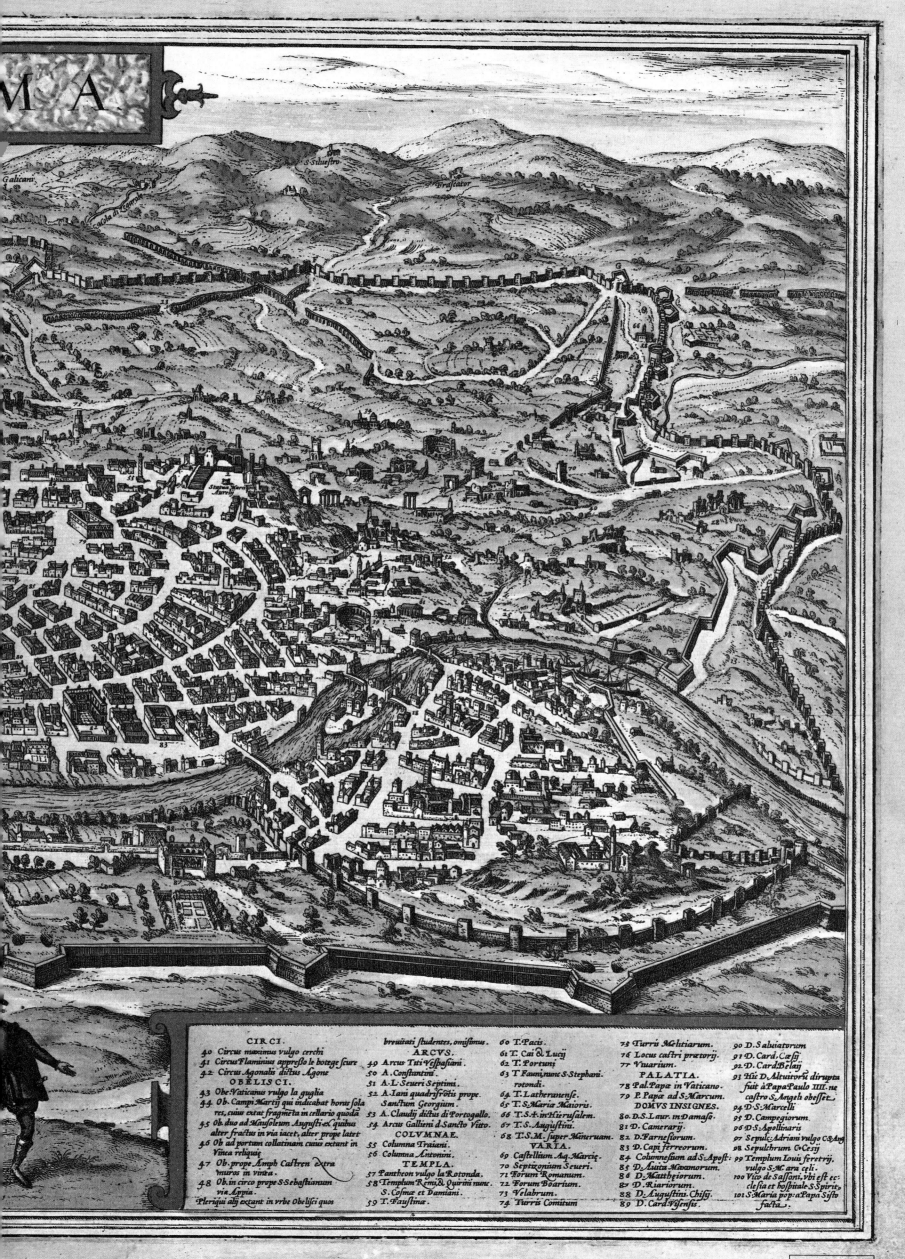

7	S. Bartolomeo vechio monast.	19	S. M.ª dll misericordia	31	S. Rocco	43	S. Allo
8	S. Maria noua	20	S. Spirito	32	S. Agostino	44	S. Giouani decola
9	S. Catarina	21	S. Primian	33	S. Zeno	45	S.to Chrispino.
10	S. Tauolo	22	S. Georgio	34	S. Iacob		
11	S. Antonio	23	S. Pietro	35	La nociata osp.		
12	S. Sebastiano	24	S. Dnico	36	S. Francesco zocoli		
13	Lospitale dll c.ª dla morte	25	La Incoronata	37	S. Martino		
14	S. Anna	26	S. Gilio	38	S. Maria bel verde		
15	S. Franc.º	27	S. M.ª dla Piaza	39	S. Marco		
16	Lospitale vechio	28	S. M.ª misericº e morte	40	S. Lucia		
17	S. Pelegrino	29	S. Nicolao	41	S. Claudio badia		
18	S. Nestasia	30	Il corpo d' Xpo	42	S. Giouanni		

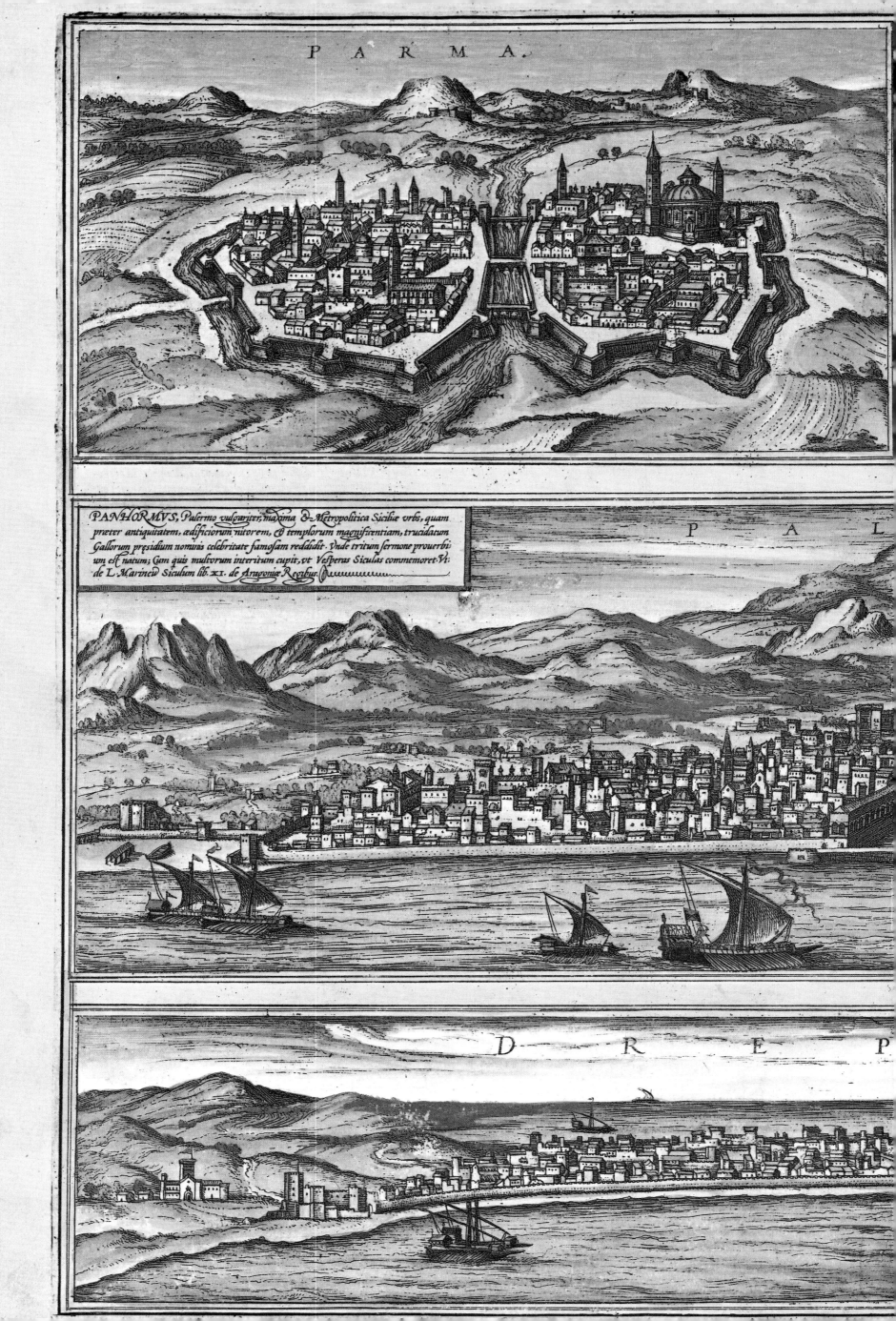

PARMA.

PANHORMVS, *Palermo vulgariter, maxima & Metropolitica Siciliæ vrbs, quam prieter antiquitatem, ædificiorum nitorem, & templorum magnificentiam, trucidatum Gallorum præsidium nominis celebritate famosam reddidit. Vnde tritum sermone prouerbium est natum; Cum quis multorum interitum cupit, vt Vesperas Siculas commemoret. Vide L. Marineus Siculum lib. XI. de Aragoniæ Regibus.*

PAL

D R E P

SENA.

El Carmini   Laiola

Torre del Pubblico
di Signori   Domo
                        Settimi
                        mo
Francesco   Monnasterio

Palazo di Sandui
                  Citadella
Forti de li Imperiali   Pallazzo del
                              Giuoli

ERMO.

A   N   V   M.

Cum Privilegio

XXVIII

CVSCO

MEXICO.

MEXICO REGIA ET CELEBRIS HISPANIÆ NOVAE CIVITAS

CUS CO.

CVSCO, REGNI PERV
IN NOVO ORBE CAPVT

XXIX